FA
PHENO

THE LORD OF
THE RINGS

EDITED BY
LORNA PIATTI-FARNELL

Credits

First published in the UK in 2015 by Intellect Books,
The Mill, Parnall Road, Fishponds, Bristol, BS16 3JG, UK

First published in the USA in 2015 by Intellect Books,
The University of Chicago Press, 1427 E. 60th Street,
Chicago, IL 60637, USA

Editor: Lorna Piatti-Farnell

Series Editor and Design: Gabriel Solomons

Typesetting: Stephanie Sarlos

Copy Editor: Emma Rhys

A catalogue record for this book is available from
the British Library

Fan Phenomena Series
ISSN: 2051-4468
eISSN: 2051-4476

Fan Phenomena: The Lord of the Rings
ISBN: 978-1-78320-515-8
eISBN: 978-1-78320-516-5

Printed and bound by
Bell & Bain Limited, Glasgow

🄡 intellect

Contents

Acknowledgements

First and foremost, I would like to thank Gabriel Solomons, the Fan Phenomena series editor at Intellect, who continued to show an interest in a project on *The Lord of the Rings*, and kept in touch with me about editing the book. Warm thanks go to the contributors of this collection, who worked tirelessly on delivering exciting and fascinating chapters.

I am grateful to my colleagues and students at Auckland University of Technology, who often asked me about the project, indulged my obsession with *The Lord of the Rings*, and afforded me a joke or two when I really needed it. I am also very grateful to Shayne Forrest, the marketing manager at Hobbiton Movie Set Tours in Mata Mata, New Zealand, who responded to my queries promptly and gave me permission to use their wonderful promotional photographs.

The most heartfelt thanks go, naturally, to my friends and family, for supporting me throughout the project and for keeping my spirits up. Particular thanks go to Colette and Richard Wood, who always show the most heart-warming interest for anything that I'm working on. And, as ever, my greatest gratitude goes to my husband, Rob Farnell, who is always there for me, every step of the way.

Lorna Piatti-Farnell, Editor

Introduction : The Fans of the Rings
Lorna Piatti-Farnell

→ Over the decades, J. R. R. Tolkien's *The Lord of the Rings* (1954–55) has established its position in the readers' minds as the 'quintessential fantasy' narrative (Walters 3). Together with their predecessor *The Hobbit* (1937), the books have gathered an impressive fandom following, and continued to enjoy immense popularity in the wider cultural scope.

Figure 1: The theatrical poster for The Lord of the Rings: The Fellowship of the Ring © 2001, New Line Cinema.

Ever since Peter Jackson first released his film adaptations of Tolkien's beloved books, *The Lord of the Rings* film trilogy (2001, 2002, 2003) has also become a household name in the world of fandom, as well as an utterly unavoidable example of fantasy cinema.

Winner of multiple awards – including many Academy Awards – *The Lord of the Rings* trilogy is a real popular culture icon. The trilogy is now, arguably, one of the most recognizable cinematic series in the world; Jackson's films have catapulted *The Lord of the Rings* narratives to the mainstream, and there are probably very few people who do not know what a 'hobbit' or an 'orc' is.

From the early days of the trilogy's success, director Peter Jackson showed a clear desire and sophisticated ability to capture the attention of potential fans: mixing technology with a pre-established interest in the subject, Jackson took advantage of the power of 'the Internet' to engage existing fans of Tolkien's books – and whet their appetite for the films – as well as to recruit potential new followers for the narrative. Jackson's involvement with important online sources such as *TheOneRing.net* opened immense possibilities for the reach of the film trilogy by capitalizing on 'active' and 'participatory' fans (see Jenkins), who often feel a sense of ownership for the final product, and perceive they should have a say in the creative development of the Tolkien universe. Over the years, multiple websites have provided a venue for fans to maintain clear and live connections with the films as a developing franchise, as well as their production, circulation, and reception. The very term 'fan' here is taken to mean both readers and viewers who display a deep connection with the product, and feel they are invested in ways that go beyond casual watching, even if those casual watchers like the movies very much. The 'fans of the rings' do not simply 'like' *The Lord of the Rings* – often affectionately known as *LOTR*: they show a desire to be involved, to comment, to speculate, and, given the opportunity, to become part of the narrative of Middle-earth.

It is no longer a surprise to hear of the reimagining of the stunning landscape of New Zealand – Jackson's home country and where the trilogy was filmed – as 'Middle-earth'. The unavoidable shots of New Zealand's impressive mountains, streams and green lands were a memorable point of difference for Jackson's films, and a general sense of

Introduction
Lorna Piatti-Farnell

acceptance surrounds the idea that, as far as the cinematic version of the narrative is concerned, New Zealand *is* Middle-earth. Heavy marketing campaigns and the establishment of location tours have cemented the place occupied by the country in not only the fans' psyche, but also the collective imagination (Carl, Kindon and Smith; Jones and Smith). The fans' love for *LOTR* often overspills into obsession, as the desire to relive the fantastic narratives of Middle-earth, and feel part of 'the rings', moves followers to extend the experience of the films into other areas of their everyday life. Naturally, this aided the construction of not only *The Lord of the Rings* trilogy as a cinematic phenomenon, but also as a cultural circle with its own distinct 'fan phenomena'.

And while the recent *Hobbit* films (Peter Jackson, 2012, 2013, 2014) have generally failed to generate such devoted fan-interest, *The Lord of the Rings* trilogy continues to appeal. From fanfiction to fan-made movies, location tours of 'Hobbiton' and celebrity worshipping, the devoted fans of the trilogy do it all. It is therefore important to address the reach of *The Lord of the Rings* – not only the books, but most noticeably their cinematic counterparts – in the world of fandom, and assess its effects on the viewers and their ways of life. *Fan Phenomena: The Lord of the Rings* does precisely this: it delves into the philosophy of the 'fans of the rings', and explores the multifaceted nuances of the *LOTR* fan community, as preoccupations with genre, stardom, and authenticity are thrown into sharp relief.

The first chapter of the collection, 'Making Fantasy Matter: *The Lord of the Rings* and the Legitimization of Fantasy Cinema' by Alexander Sergeant, sets the scene for understanding Peter Jackson's trilogy as part of fantasy cinema, and validating its value as a visual medium. Sergeant explores how *The Lord of the Rings* did not simply remind viewers that fantasy 'existed', but also proved that the genre can be treated just as seri-

Figure 2: The tourist information site in Mata Mata, New Zealand, where the Hobbiton Movie Set Tours is located. Particularly worthy of note is the effort made to recreate the style of the hobbits' town buildings in Peter Jackson's cinematic versions of the story ©2015, Lorna Piatti-Farnell.

Figure 3: A 'hobbit hole' as presented on the Hobbiton Movie Set Tour in New Zealand ©2015 Hobbiton Movie Set Tours.

ously as any other popular form of film-making. Chapter 2, '*The Lord of the Rings*: One Digital Fandom to Initiate Them All' by Maggie Parke, explores the activities of the film-makers of *The Lord of the Rings*, and their interactions with their fans. Parke sees creators of the trilogy as pioneers into the complex realm of the management of event films and their fan bases, with a particular emphasis on digital platforms.

In Chapter 3, 'Reforging the Rings: Fan Edits and the Cinematic Middle-earth', Joshua Wille explores the popular practices of fans creating their own 'fan edits' of *LOTR* narratives. Wille perceives fan edits as individual artistic expressions, articulations of personal readings, and a means for fans to manifest the movies they want to see. The expanding field of *LOTR* fan editing is providing appealing reinterpretations of a film series that epitomizes an already revisionist mode in contemporary cinema. In similar fashion, Chapter 4, 'Walking Between Two Lands, or How Double Canon Works in *The Lord of the Rings* Fan Films' by Miguel Ángel Pérez-Gómez, explores *LOTR* 'fan films' in relation to the idea of narrative canon. Pérez-Gómez surveys how, in the world of *The Lord of the Rings* fandom, fan films are informed by two distinct but interconnected canons: the fictional universe set up by Tolkien, on the one hand, and the aesthetics created by Peter Jackson, on the other.

The practice of visiting New Zealand film locations and sets as part of a 'fan experience' of *The Lord of the Rings* is the centre of editor Lorna Piatti-Farnell's own contribution in this volume: Chapter 5, entitled 'On Party Business: True-fan Celebrations in New Zealand's Middle-earth', explores the movie set of Hobbiton in New Zealand as a fansite connected to a sense of community, identification, and the search for the 'real' Middle-earth. Piatti-Farnell places a particular emphasis on the fans' propensity to host *LOTR*-themed parties in Hobbiton, and what the implications of such a practice are, in social, cultural, and even economic terms. The fans' search for Middle-earth is also explored by Emily Gray in Chapter 6, 'There, Here, and Back Again: The Search for Middle-earth in Birmingham'. Gray, however, distances herself from the contemporary

Introduction
Lorna Piatti-Farnell

view of New Zealand as the land of *The Lord of the Rings*, and traces Tolkien's connection to Birmingham (UK), mapping the narrative and iconography of the books on this particular city instead.

The impact of fandom and fan practices on the perception of *The Lord of the Rings* narratives is pursued by Cait Coker and Karen Viars in Chapter 7, 'Looking for Lothiriel: The Presence of Women in Tolkien Fandom'. Coker and Cairs explore the depiction of Tolkien's and Jackson's female characters in *The Lord of the Rings* through the lens of fanfiction: fan-written poems and short stories that extend the life of little-known characters such as Lothiriel are surveyed in order to scope how these reinterpretations propose a 'new' picture of the women of Middle-earth. The notions of 'appropriation' and 're-adaptation' are also relevant to Chapter 8, Paul Mountfort's contribution to the volume entitled 'Lord of the Franchise: *The Lord of the Rings*, IP Rights and Policing Appropriation'. Mountfort, however, focuses on the copyright 'battles' that have been the centre of many adaptations of Tolkien's work, particularly in the case of Jackson's cinematic version. Starting from copyright events that date back to even before Tolkien's death, and drawing on his own experience of dealing with what he terms the intellectual property 'battlefields', Mountfort surveys the difficulties encountered by potential fan authors when drawing on inevitably influential *LOTR* mythology for their works.

The last two chapters of the collection extend the look into fandom 'beyond' the *LOTR* texts, and explore notions of celebrity worshipping, and the reception of 'other' narratives from the Tolkien-based cinematic universe, such as *The Hobbit* (Peter Jackson, 2012, 2013, 2014). In Chapter 9, 'Writing the Star: *The Lord of the Rings* and the Production of Star Narratives', Anna Martin looks at the marketing of *The Lord of the Rings* star Viggo Mortensen – and his role as 'Aragorn' – via media venues that have capitalized on the combination of DVD technology, the expansion of broadband Internet and user-based content, and the development of celebrity culture as we know it today. Martin contends that the Viggo Mortensen case study shows the evolution of a new model of star marketing, based on a perceived sense of familiarity and intimacy with the fans. The book concludes with Chapter 10, 'Understanding Fans' "Precious": The Impact of *The Lord of the Rings* Films on the *Hobbit* Movies', where contributor Abigail G. Scheg claims that it was the rampant success of *The Lord of the Rings* movies that made it impossible for the *Hobbit* movies to be as successful a film endeavour. Aware of the fact that *The Hobbit* never really reached the levels of popularity of its *LOTR* predecessor, Scheg discusses different fan expectations of the *Hobbit* films and analyses the ways in which these prequel films met and disappointed fans of Tolkien's work.

For readers who are particularly interested in exploring the connections between Tolkien's works and Jackson's cinematic renditions of both *The Lord of the Rings* and *The Hobbit*, the book also includes an interview with Shaun Gunner, the president of the Tolkien Society. Gunner provides intriguing insights into the reception and perception of Jackson's film within the Tolkien fan community, and provides a successful bridge in joining the multiple facets of the fan experience of these works, and the various practices and 'phenomena' that surround it. ●

~~~~~~~~~~

GO FURTHER

Books

Fantasy Film: A Critical Introduction
James Walters
(Oxford: Berg, 2011)

Textual Poachers: Television Fans and Participatory Culture
Henry Jenkins
(New York: Routledge, 1992)

Extracts/Essays/Articles

'Tourists' Experiences of Film Locations: New Zealand as "*Middle-Earth*"'
Daniela Carl, Sara Kindon and Karen Smith
In *Tourism Geographies: An International Journal of Tourism Space, Place and Environment*. 9: 1 (2007), pp. 49–63.

'Middle-earth Meets New Zealand: Authenticity and Location in the Making of *The Lord of the Rings*'
Deborah Jones and Karen Smith
In *Journal of Management Studies*. 42: 5 (2005), pp. 923–45.

'Fantasy, Franchises, and Frodo Baggins: *The Lord of the Rings* and Modern Hollywood'
Kristin Thompson
In *The Velvet Light Trap*. 52 (2003), pp. 45–63.

Chapter
01

Making Fantasy Matter: *The Lord of the Rings* and the Legitimization of Fantasy Cinema

Alexander Sergeant

→ In the past decade, the Hollywood fantasy film has established itself as arguably the twenty-first century's most popular form of film-making, a feat made all the more remarkable given the genre's somewhat troubled critical and commercial history. Exemplified in a number of high-profile examples scattered throughout Hollywood's history, including *Doctor Dolittle* (Richard Fleischer, 1967), *Willow* (Ron Howard, 1988) and *Hook* (Steven Spielberg, 1991), the fantasy film has traditionally been met with a mixture of apathy from mainstream audiences and derision from traditional newspaper and magazine critics.

This attitude showed no signs of changing at the dawn of a new millennium when *Dungeons and Dragons* (Courtney Solomon, 2000) was released internationally to both critical and commercial disappointment, described by A. O. Scott in the *New York Times* as a 'noisy, nerve-racking tedium of contemporary popular culture'. Yet, the release of New Line Cinema's adaptation of *The Lord of the Rings* would witness a fundamental change in the attitudes of both audiences and critics towards an oft-dismissed genre of film-making. Breaking box office records and opening to enthusiastic reviews worldwide, *The Lord of the Rings* not only ushered in a new era of the Hollywood fantasy franchise but was held up by journalists and critics such as Kenneth Turan as a model 'for how to bring substance, authenticity and insight to the biggest of adventure yarns'. Self-conscious in their desire to remove the films from the pejorative stigma long-associated with the fantasy genre, producers and screenwriters Boyes, Jackson and Walsh pioneered a number of formal and stylistic features that would not only prove hugely influential for future fantasy franchises, but would encourage audiences to look at the various trolls, wizards and hobbits presented in such stories in an entirely new way. The trilogy managed to showcase the merits of fantasy to a traditional intellectual establishment. By taking fantasy seriously, the trilogy's popularity seemed to come hand in hand with a new era of critical legitimacy.

Part of the reason the creative team behind *The Lord of the Rings* trilogy was able to legitimize the fantasy genre in this manner was due to the literary prestige of the source novel. Prior to the release of the trilogy, Hollywood adapted fantasy films from pulp fiction or comic book sources which, although popular amongst certain subsections of US culture, lacked the necessary prestige to register amongst mainstream audiences. Films such as *Conan the Barbarian* (John Milius, 1982) had managed to achieve a modest degree of financial success, but were primarily designed to appeal to a specialist audience of self-conscious fantasy fans rather than the broader audiences courted by Hollywood studios. In contrast, *The Lord of the Rings* was a film franchise targeted at the same audiences who, throughout the 1980s and 1990s, had been raised on a steady diet of action and science fiction cinema. Producers hoped that the phenomenal cultural impact Tolkien's novel had made not only within the United States but around the globe would allow it to transcend the specialist or niche appeal that fantasy film-making had enjoyed up until this point, and allow the film trilogy to succeed where countless others had failed.

Occupying a prominent position within the canon of twentieth-century English literature and frequently discussed by literary scholars for its remarkable depth of vision in the creation of Middle-earth, Tolkien's novel reflects the moral and ethical concerns of a practising Roman Catholic writing during a time of world war and the invention of the atomic bomb. In his own essay of literary criticism, 'On Fairy Stories' (1947), Tolkien advocated that writers should utilize the supernatural not as an 'end to itself' but instead as a device whose virtue lies 'in its operations' (11). Screenwriters Boyes, Jackson and Walsh sought to follow this example in adapting Tolkien's narrative to the big screen by emphasizing the angst-ridden plot embedded with the original story. The trilogy condenses

Making Fantasy Matter: *The Lord of the Rings* and the Legitimization of Fantasy Cinema
Alexander Sergeant

Tolkien's epic tale to focus primarily on Frodo and Sam's journey to Mount Doom and the threat posed by Sauron due to the survival of the One Ring. Frodo is presented largely as a substance addict, and his fate is continually juxtaposed with the now-iconic character of Gollum whose status as a tragic antagonist is invested with a certain degree of psychological realism. Characters such as Boromir in *The Fellowship of the Ring* (2001) and Faramir in *The Two Towers* (2002) spend the majority of their time on-screen gripped in a self-destructive torment, whilst Aragon's decision whether or not to accept the throne of Gondor is given greater emphasis from the minor subplot it serves in the original novel. Whimsical episodes such as 'The House of Tom Bombadil' or the encounter with Old Man Willow are all but removed from the cinematic adaptation, and what is emphasized above all else is a feeling of dread and mortality. The narrative of *The Lord of the Rings* exemplifies a desire to be taken seriously, and to move the fantasy genre away from the pejorative connotations amassed by many of its previous forays on-screen.

Figure 1: A still from The Wizard of Oz demonstrating that the way in which the use of Technicolor, costume and set design are combined together in classical Hollywood fantasy films often invites visual spectacle through an exoticization of their magical imagery © Metro-Goldwyn-Meyer, 1939

Beyond these decisions taken at the level of character and narrative, the way in which Jackson depicts Middle-earth is also marked by a desire to dissociate *The Lord of the Rings* from a kind of visual spectacle offered in previous fantasy films. Whilst previous fantasy films had invited audiences to gaze at the otherworldliness of that which was on-screen – Dorothy's famous entrance into Munchkinland in *The Wizard of Oz* (Victor Fleming, 1939) being a prime example of this kind of aesthetic (Figure 1) – *The Lord of the Rings* is primarily invested in a very different kind of visual spectacle altogether. As David Butler argues in his book *Fantasy Cinema* (2009), there is a 'marked difference' between the way in which the world of Middle-earth is brought to life on-screen in comparison with previous fantasy worlds such as Oz, or indeed the alternative fantasy worlds of *The Dark Crystal* (Jim Henson and Kathryn Oz, 1982) or *Legend* (Ridley Scott, 1985). As Kristin Thompson argues in *The Frodo Franchise* (2007), Jackson's trilogy is notable by the way in which it 'would follow Tolkien in treating the story as history rather than as fantasy' (90). Following on from Tolkien's preference to describe *The Lord of the Rings* as a work of faux history rather than as a work of fantasy, the desire to historicize fantasy manifests itself as a persistent formal and stylistic concern throughout Jackson's trilogy. This trait not only affects the way in which the story is told on-screen, but the way in which audiences are invited to respond to it.

In sequences wherein new locations are introduced to the audience for the first time, a recurrent technique occurs in which Middle-earth is made spectacular without exoticising the world on-screen. Instead, individual characters are made to seem miniscule in comparison with the vastness of the circumstances they enter (Figure 2). It is a sense of scale, rather than a sense of magic, that is placed up on-screen for our viewing pleasure; a scale that is then emphasized in the editing patterns as the scenes often cut between the subjective vantage-point of characters to impersonal panoramas designed to allow

audiences to take in the authenticity of detail achieved on-screen. This technique of the 'spectacular vista' is argued by Tom Brown to be a prominent feature of historical epics such as *Gone with the Wind* (Victor Fleming, 1939), and is defined largely by the ability of such moments to utilize visual spectacle as a device that 'vivifies or actualizes the sense of a character's relationship to the world constructed around them' (159–61). Whether it be the famous crane shot of the siege of Atlanta in *Gone with the Wind* or else the numerous shots of the Roman Colloseum in a more recent historical epic such as *Gladiator* (Ridley Scott, 2000), the spectacular vista serves to employ visual spectacle to bring the past to life in a visceral way on-screen. It is this actualization that is also presented during such key moments throughout *The Lord of the Rings* trilogy, represented perhaps most acutely in the various epic battles of Helm's Deep in *The Two Towers* and Pelennor Fields in *The Return of the King* (2003), which relied on set pieces far more in keeping with historical sagas such as *Zulu* (Cy Endfield, 1964) and *Braveheart* (Mel Gibson, 1995) than they did remind audiences of previous fantasy films. By consistently presenting fantasy in this manner, *The Lord of the Rings* subverts a certain kind of response to the supernatural on-screen and presents Tolkien's Middle-earth as a largely historicized world where visual pleasure is obtained through a series of formal and stylistic conventions, associated with historical sagas and action set-pieces that proved popular with audiences throughout the 1990s.

Having historicized Tolkien's fantasy world, *The Lord of the Rings* manages to achieve a level of naturalism on-screen which it then utilizes at key moments to invite the audience to ponder the allegorical and metaphorical ramifications of the narrative. An example of such a device can be found in a speech made by Gandalf within the Mines of Moria in *The Fellowship of the Ring*, wherein a close-up shot of Ian McKellen staring almost directly at the camera is utilized in a manner akin to the Ancient Greek theatrical device of the chorus (Figure 3). An iconic moment from the first film, the speech is given a universal quality as Gandalf stares at Frodo but also seemingly beyond the screen and into the auditorium, as if to invite audience members to ponder over the wider thematic ramifications of what he is saying. Repeated at the film's denouement, this moment serves to provide *The Fellowship of the Ring* with a thematic resolution beyond the literal circumstances taking place on-screen. Similar moments appear throughout the trilogy. Toward the end of *The Two Towers*, Sam compares the journey he and Frodo find themselves on to 'the great stories [...] the ones that really mattered', a speech that functions to unite the various story-strands together as Sam's voice-over provides a conclusion to the second instalment of the franchise (Figure 4). At the end of *The Return of the King*, Frodo himself is seen writing a copy of *The Lord of the Rings*, and reflects on the nature of the telling of his own story in

Making Fantasy Matter: *The Lord of the Rings* and the Legitimization of Fantasy Cinema
Alexander Sergeant

a manner that posits him simultaneously as protagonist and narrator. In each of these moments, the films self-consciously invite their audiences to find a figurative or metaphorical meaning for *The Lord of the Rings* beyond the specifics of Middle-earth; to interpret the trilogy as something more than a 'mere' adventure story about hobbits and orcs.

We can relate these devices to a key strategy found within fantasy literature discussed by Farah Mendlesohn. In *Rhetorics of Fantasy* (2008), Mendlesohn subdivides fantasy literature into four categories: 'the portal-quest fantasy', 'the immersive fantasy', 'the intrusion fantasy' and 'the liminal fantasy'. Mendlesohn's first three categories can broadly be defined through a series of rhetorical strategies designed to at least partially convince the reader that the supernatural components of the story are real. However, what distinguishes Mendlesohn's category of the liminal fantasy narrative is that it 'estranges' the reader from the supernatural story in a manner that allows our experience of the narrative to reach a point wherein 'metaphor and magic become indistinguishable' (195). Such a liminal approach to fantasy fiction appears in Jackson's *The Lord of the Rings*, albeit contained within certain key scenes rather than appearing as a coherent narrational strategy. One example of such a moment occurs halfway through *The Two Towers*, wherein the wizard Saruman delivers a speech to his army of uruk-hai soldiers. Not only is the speech itself reminiscent of numerous real-life speeches made by charismatic twentieth-century leaders such as Adolf Hitler, but the film invites such an interpretation through the way in which the scene juxtaposes close-up shots of the single figure of Saruman and the spectacular images of a uniformed army of soldiers (Figure 5). Reminiscent of some of the scenes from Leni Riefenstahl's *Triumph des Willens/Triumph of the Will* (1935), such moments have seemingly encouraged critics such as Richard Corliss of *Time* magazine to interpret *The Lord of the Rings* as 'a metaphor for the Allies' battle against Hitler [...] or, for that matter, the U.S. and the Northern Alliance against Osama bin Laden and the Taliban'. As Frances Pheasant-Kelly states in *Fantasy Film Post 9/11* (2013), the trilogy invited spectators to engage with the narrative framed through a perspective of 'shared global histories' that ranged from the imagery of the Holocaust in the gaunt figure of Gollum to images of 9/11 evoked through the spectacle of warfare (25). By deliberately inviting such comparisons in the way in which certain scenes and characters are presented, *The Lord of the Rings* utilizes the supernatural as a device that those who are willing can use as a springboard for their own interpretation, allowing them a whole new life beyond that which is on-screen.

David Hartwell's essay 'Dollars and Dragons' (1996) pinpoints Tolkien's work as the epochal novel of modern fantasy literature, its success inspiring numerous imitators both conscious and unconscious of its influence in a manner that sculpted an understanding of the genre for decades to come. The same influential impact might also be attributed to its cinematic adaptations. The critical re-appraisal that Jackson's trilogy would achieve for the fantasy genre would culminate inside Los Angeles's Kodak Theatre on 29 February 2004. Having already won ten Academy Awards that same evening for the film's achieve-

Figure 4: 'It's like in the great stories, Mr Frodo, the ones that really mattered.' Samwise ruminates on the moral ramifications of his own story in The Lord of the Rings: The Two Towers © New Line Cinema, 2002.

Figure 5: Juxtaposing the single image of Saruman with the faceless army of orcs, *The Lord of the Rings: The Two Towers* is reminiscent in its visual style of Leni Riefenstahl's *Triumph of the Will* and, as such, invites comparisons between the fantasy narrative of The Lord of the Rings and real-life twentieth-century events © New Line Cinema, 2002 and © Reichsparteitag Film, 1935.

ments in screenwriting and visual effects, *The Return of the King* crowned its success by becoming the first fantasy film to win the coveted statue of Best Picture. On this occasion, the trilogy's co-writer, co-producer and director Peter Jackson took to the stage to deliver his take on the shift occurring in fantasy's critical recognition. As Jackson stated:

> I'm so honoured, touched and relieved that the academy, and the members of the academy, that have supported us have seen past the trolls and the wizards and the hobbits and are recognizing fantasy this year. Fantasy is an F-word that, hopefully, the five-second delay won't do anything with.

Greeted by warm laughter inside the theatre, Jackson's comments reveal not only an awareness on the part of the creative team behind *The Lord of the Rings* of the somewhat dismissive attitude their choice of genre had received in the years prior to their decision to adapt Tolkien's novel, but also indicate a key strategy by which the films themselves attempted to circumnavigate such opinions. *The Lord of the Rings* was to prove a pivotal film that fundamentally altered both the way in which fantasy would be presented on-screen, and the kind of response it invited from such supernatural imagery. It invited us to 'see past' the hobbits through a series of formal and stylistic strategies that not only normalized the potentially hyperbolic or bathetic nature of fantasy on-screen but also courted a series of metaphorical interpretations in that process. As we continue to 'see past' hobbits, so too fantasy ceases to be the F-word it once was amongst both film academia and popular culture. ●

GO FURTHER

Books

Fantasy Film Post 9/11
Frances Pheasant-Kelly
(New York: Palgrave MacMillan, 2013)

Fantasy Cinema: Impossible Worlds on Screen
David Butler
(London: Wallflower Press, 2009)

Making Fantasy Matter: *The Lord of the Rings* and the Legitimization of Fantasy Cinema
Alexander Sergeant

Rhetorics of Fantasy
Farah Mendlesohn
(Middletown, CT: Wesleyan University Press, 2008)

The Frodo Franchise: 'The Lord of the Rings' and Modern Hollywood
Kristin Thompson
(Berkeley, CA: University of California Press, 2007)

Extracts/Essays/Articles

'Spectacle/Gender/History: The Case of *Gone with the Wind*'
Tom Brown
In *Screen*. 49: 2 (2008), pp. 157-78.

'Dollars and Dragons: The Truth about Fantasy'
David G. Hartwell
In David G. Hartwell. *Age of Wonders: Exploring the World of Science-fiction* (New York:
Tom Doherty Associates Inc., 1996), pp. 304-31.

'On Fairy Stories'
J. R. R. Tolkien
In Christopher Tolkien (ed.). *The Monsters and the Critics and Other Essays* (London:
George Allen & Unwin Publishers Ltd., [1947] 1983), pp. 10-22.

Online

'Movie Review'
Kenneth Turan
Los Angeles Times. 16 April 2003, http://articles.latimes.com/2003/dec/16/entertain-
ment/et-turan16.

'Lord of the Films'
Richard Corliss
Time. 17 December 2001, http://www.time.com/time/world/article/0,8599,188807,00.
html.

'After D&D you may need R&R'
A. O. Scott
The New York Times. 8 December 2000, http://www.nytimes.com/2000/12/08/
arts/08DUNG.html.

Films

The Lord of the Rings: The Return of the King, Peter Jackson, dir. (USA: Wingnut/New Line, 2003).

The Lord of the Rings: The Two Towers, Peter Jackson, dir. (USA: Wingnut/New Line, 2002).

The Lord of the Rings: The Fellowship of the Ring, Peter Jackson, dir. (USA: Wingnut/New Line, 2001).

Dungeons and Dragons, Courtney Solomon, dir. (USA: New Line, 2000).

Gladiator, Ridley Scott, dir. (USA: Scott Free Productions, 2000).

Braveheart, Mel Gibson, dir. (USA: Icon Productions, 1995).

Hook Steven Spielberg, dir. (USA: Amblin Entertainment, 1991).

Willow, Ron Howard, dir. (USA: Lucasfilm, 1988).

Legend, Ridley Scott, dir. (USA: Universal, 1985).

Conan the Barbarian, John Milius, dir. (USA: Dino de Laurentiis Corporation, 1982).

The Dark Crystal, Jim Henson and Frank Oz, dirs (UK/USA: ITC Entertainment, 1982).

Doctor Dolittle, Richard Liescher, dir. (USA: Apjac Productions, 1967).

Zulu, Cy Endfield, dir. (UK: Diamond Films, 1964).

Gone with the Wind, Victor Fleming, dir. (USA: Selznick International Pictures, 1939).

The Wizard of Oz, Victor Fleming, dir. (USA: MGM, 1939).

Triumph des Willens/Triumph of the Will, Leni Riefenstahl, dir. (Germany: Reichsparteitag Film, 1935).

Chapter
02

The Lord of the Rings: One Digital Fandom to Initiate Them All

Maggie Parke

→ In this chapter, I will explore the activities of the film-makers of *The Lord of the Rings* directed by Peter Jackson, and their interactions with their fans, as the trilogy that pioneered the inroads into the complex realm of the management of event films and their fan bases – particularly their engagement on digital platforms. The film-makers' efforts laid the basics of fan–film-maker interaction mimicked by subsequent event films such as *Twilight* (Catherine Hardwicke, 2008), *The Hunger Games* (Gary Ross, 2012) and *Divergent* (Neil Burger, 2014).

The film-makers of *The Lord of the Rings* were relatively limited in their outreach abilities in comparison to these recent films, due to the more basic technological modes and more limited use of social interactions: Facebook did not launch until 2004, Twitter until 2006, and fans couldn't have the immediate access that they have now through constantly-connected smartphones – iPhones were not released until 2007. Instead, fans converged almost exclusively on *TheOneRing.net* (*TORn*), the leading *Lord of the Rings* fansite. As I will illustrate here, the film-makers' efforts to connect with those who managed *TORn*, and to acknowledge and work with their expectations and interact with them, helped to secure the fandom as part of the films' audience throughout the adaptation process.

One fansite to rule them all

The Internet as an interactive medium greatly shifted the relationship between fans and film-makers. Fans can now immediately access this once-unknown process that happened behind closed studio doors. They do not have to wait for their news via printed media such as fan or pop culture magazines, but instead can get instant updates from actors on Twitter, or find leaked scripts and photos from a film's set. This immediacy can provide a quick and inexpensive way to communicate with fans; however, it can also create a deluge of incorrect information and spoilers. By having film-makers participate in the sharing of information, they create the possibility of an information dam: a protected way to permit a steady but safe amount of information to the fan base, somewhat regulated by the film-making team itself.

The Lord of the Rings was ahead of the curve, considering this online activity took place in the early days of web 2.0. Sean Astin, who played Samwise Gamgee in the films, noted that an extensive amount of their marketing consisted of Internet interaction. He said, 'there was a whole Internet strategy, [...] [which] started with Peter interacting with Harry Knowles,' who is a popular writer for the website *Ain't It Cool News*, and known for his fan-like interviews and strong online presence.

The film-makers' Internet-based activities expanded during production from marketing to fan interaction. Initially, during the early days of filming, one of the owners of *TheOneRing.net* was 'escorted off the set', as described on their site, after repeat attempts to get close to the production during its filming in New Zealand. He was, however, eventually 'graciously invited back' to meet director Peter Jackson during initial filming in 1999 and welcomed by Jackson as a fellow fan. Kristin Thompson's research on the production practices and franchise expansion of *The Lord of the Rings* investigated this experience, noting that a number of 'spies received trespass notices, but New Line – the studio behind *The Lord of the Rings* – soon realized that controlling rather than thwarting such activity would generate invaluable free publicity'. This meeting began a partnership for information sharing during the months prior to the films' release.

On their website, the owners explain their contact with the film-makers as a 'rela-

The Lord of the Rings: One Digital Fandom to Initiate Them All
Maggie Parke

tionship', and describe how that relationship, and subsequently the site, thrived during the years following filming and during the films' releases. Sean Astin also noted the pervasiveness of the fansite, and attributed much of the popular awareness of *The Lord of the Rings* to their reporting efforts and coverage. He also acknowledged his own relationship with the site creator: 'I couldn't help but be aware of a lot of the sites, and I am friends with the creator of *TheOneRing.net*.' This places the fansite in close proximity with the film-makers, and is described as 'in alliance' with them. That close relationship is then translated to the fandom via *TORn*, thereby projecting the film-makers as thoughtful and kind, and highlighting their efforts for a faithful adaptation, which encouraged the positive reception that the film-makers and their adaptation processes received from the fan base. The film-makers offered the fans exclusive information to post on *TORn*, including personal interviews, photos and breaking news regarding the adaptation. In return, the fansite was involved and incorporated into the adaptation process, making the owners and moderators key players in the films' marketing to the fans, by the fans.

Kaleb Nation is known in the *Twilight* fandom as 'the *Twilight* Guy', and is a media personality, a YouTube 'famous-face', and creator of the YouTube show, '60 Second Rant', where he dives into a fan reaction or news event of the week. His videos have millions of views, and he is a blogebrity often seen at VidCon and ComiCon. He says that, 'Fans trust fans. Filmmakers could potentially just be in it for the money, but fans get fans.' *TORn* provided extensive, positive free advertising for the film, delivered by the site owners who were trusted voices within the fandom, and often considered more reliable than the film-makers as the fansite owner has more established fan capital, and more longevity within the fandom. The site owners of *TORn* projected their good relationship with the film-makers of *The Lord of the Rings* through blog posts on their site, however, which united fans and film-makers, and also gave the studio an enthusiastic and well-informed online 'street team' composed of trusted fans, reporting to the larger fan base accurate and sanctioned information.

Aside from inviting the fansite owners onto the set in New Zealand, the film-makers sought to involve fans from all over the world in an unprecedented act of fan inclusion and cooperative marketing in the extended DVDs. These DVDs are a font of information about the specific decisions in adapting the novel to the screen, the extensive discussions and research into minute details of everything from script to prop design and costume, and as Hunter writes in his enlightening article, they 'encourage multiple viewings, absorption into the details of adaptation and film production, and allow consumers a sense of participation in the phenomenon [...] all of which help turn a blockbuster into a mass cult film' (164).

Within these extended DVDs, there was also a new marketing technique with the creation of a digital and actual film fanclub that provided financial gain, and also allowed the fans closer access to the film. To join, fans paid for their registration to *The Lord of the*

Rings fanclub, and in addition to the textual merchandise they would receive (i.e. membership card, newsletter, etc.), they could also submit their names to be included in the credits at the end of the extended edition of *The Lord of the Rings*. Actor Elijah Wood, who plays Frodo, was the first to sign up:

> I think what they're doing with the fan club is really wonderful. Since I started working on these films, I've been amazed by how many people have been impacted by this story and how much they care about it at a deep, emotional level. The fan club creates one big, worldwide society of *The Lord of the Rings* fans and I am proud to be part of that. Besides, I want to be sure Peter puts my name in the credits of the film's DVD (www.theonering.net).

By creating an interactive fanclub, which resulted in the appearance of actual participation in the film via their names in the credits, fans became a part of the process. In addition to this, the encouragement from Frodo, arguably the films' central hero, aligns him with the fans. He also jokingly levels himself as equal to the fans as he suggests joining this club is truly the only way to ensure his name is in the credits.

Film-makers as fans: Being on the same team

The film-makers were keen to work with the fans instead of against them, and actively reached out to fansite owners, invited fans on set for interviews and photo opportunities to share with the fan base, and gave them invitations to premieres, after-party events and DVD-release events as special guests. In addition to their direct interactions with the fans, the film-makers of *The Lord of the Rings* also clearly portrayed themselves as fans, perhaps in an attempt to identify and align themselves with the fan base, reinforcing Kaleb Nation's earlier quote about 'fans trusting fans'. If the film-makers could be seen as fans, they could provide an element of their own personality that is relatable to the average fan through their connection with the source novel, and it might illustrate a passion for the text that the fan could relate to and appreciate.

For example, in *The Lord of the Rings* cast, Sir Ian McKellen, who played the wizard Gandalf, adapted his personal website to include information about the films in one of the earliest online blogs by a well-known and respected actor in a popular event-film adaptation. Here, in a blog he titled *The Grey Book* after his character Gandalf the Grey, he provided details about the set up of the scene both in the script and his own performance in all three films. Once they gained a significant readership, he reorganized the site so that the posts now appear chronologically, as he initially wrote them at the beginning of 1999. He acknowledged this change and spoke about it directly to the fans: 'I hope reading them in or out of order will convey the fascination and excitement [of the process],' encouraging fan engagement. He later added a *Gandalf the White* section, which are posts written after 2002, following the worldwide success of *The Fellowship of the Ring* (2001).

Figure 2: Peter Jackson is often depicted as hobbit-like, including at premieres and press events, ©2014, Creative Commons.

Figures 3 and 4: Original art of Hobbiton, and the film's depiction of it, ©1954 and 2012, Creative Commons.

This first-hand account allows fans closer access to the process, and depicts McKellen as an avid fan of the production himself.

Aside from McKellen, I. Q. Hunter notes that various other actors were depicted as fans in multiple ways. Director Peter Jackson was seen as 'a genial, tubby, bare-footed hobbit' (157) and was photographed for promotional material looking hobbit-like, smoking his hobbit pipe, and looking every bit a hobbit as any ComiCon cosplay attendee. Additionally, on McKellen's blog, he described Jackson as committed to fansite observation: 'I don't know where Peter gets the time but he seems to be au fait with the Tolkien sites and often refers to them in detail.' McKellen admitted to visiting the sites anonymously, and that he was 'sometimes tempted to correct the wilder speculations in the correspondence columns [...] [but] I keep quiet. And so, it seems, does Peter' (www.mckellen.com). Although this does not necessarily mean that Jackson was online, interacting with his fans, it projects a media creator who makes an effort to keep the Internet as a part of his life, as does the digital fan, and who understands the loyal fans' desire for information.

The film-makers' interest in the novels, and their apparent passion for the project, is also visible in the rest of the cast. One can't be certain if they are *sincerely* this passionate, but the *appearance* of it is key; it may alleviate fans' concern and panic as they can relate to the film-makers and trust their actions as fellow fans. Through the actors' commentary on the extended DVDs (2004), it is easy to see how familiar they are with the text. They are able to recall minute details from the Appendices of Tolkien's novels, such as when Billy Boyd comments on his character's son marrying Sam's daughter, or the history of the elves from Tolkien's creation story, *The Silmarillion* (1977). I also asked Sean Astin in an e-mail (2014) if he read the books prior to being cast, and if he re-read them during filming and he answered, 'Yes. All of the above. We re-read them constantly [...] they became a sacred text for us throughout the film.' This projects their dedicated and passionate interaction with the text, like that of a fan.

Visual expectations: One vision to unite them all

Jackson's *LOTR* films were also good at matching fans' visual expectations of Middle-earth, as prior to filming, Peter Jackson hired artists Alan Lee and John Howe to create the concept art for the film. Their art was familiar to the fan base and has been consistently associated with Tolkien's work, as Alan Lee illustrated the anniversary editions of *The Hobbit* and *The Lord of the Rings* in 1991, and John Howe illustrated the 1991 calendar. Co-producer Rick Porras noted that it was

well documented how Alan [Lee] and John [Howe] were well-versed in the worlds of Middle Earth [...] they were a perfect combo who would not only do their own design, but also drift amongst the team making comments and giving inspiration.

Alan Lee, in Sibley's seminal work, commented on Jackson's use of him and his art for the film trilogy and said, 'I was impressed by the fact that he wanted to be true to the spirit of the books and try to create a believable world with real landscapes and places.' Lee was originally needed for just twelve to twenty weeks, but instead stayed on the project for a total of three years, thus connecting the visions of Tolkien with the visual reinterpretation of the films. These efforts provided the visual manifestation of a fan's perceived depiction of Middle-earth, and provided an easy transition of the imagined world of the text to the realized world of the film. McKellan wrote of their involvement on his blog, and assisted in continuing the positive impression of the fan-like dedication of the production team, reinforcing the importance of Tolkien in the process and including the vital role of Howe and Lee in creating his character:

> Peter Jackson has ensured that Tolkien rules the enterprise. So, in working out Gandalf's appearance we went back to the few terse descriptions in the novel. We agreed that the cover illustration of Gandalf on the Harper Collins complete edition of *The Lord of the Rings* had captured too much of our collective imaginings to be ignored. John Howe painted it and he has for 18 months been crucial to the 'conceptual art' of the movie, along with that other formidably imaginative illustrator, Alan Lee.

Discussion boards had largely positive fan reactions to the film-makers' efforts to meet fan expectations of *The Lord of the Rings* with comments on message boards like, 'kudos to the folks at New Line for creating a masterpiece worthy of Tolkien's world and words', and this also gave an opportunity for fans to establish fan hierarchy through fanspeak:

> I spotted the stone trolls (circa *Hobbit*) [...] Who else picked up on the subtle touches? Let's share – me first: Whenever Frodo looks at the Ruling Ring, the voice he hears is saying the engraved incantation in Mordor speak.

These comments illustrate positive fan reaction, and also elements of criticism or discovery that fans use to illustrate fan capital – their shared discoveries within the film that relate to insider knowledge from the books, the adaptation process and the films.

Conclusion: A fan management process for all?
All of these elements – from film-makers as fans, to fan recognition of visual depictions of the fictional world – may not necessarily make the film successful, but it supports the

The Lord of the Rings: **One Digital Fandom to Initiate Them All**
Maggie Parke

argument that it does not harm the film financially. *The Fellowship of the Ring* made $90.3 million in its opening weekend and $968.7 million in the worldwide box office, as seen in the table below. The financial evidence and the anecdotal reactions from the fans are highly suggestive that the audiences drawn to the film were large, widespread, and most likely saw the film more than once, suggesting that the fans were satisfied and enjoyed the film.

Film	Budget	Opening Weekend	Worldwide Box Office	US Box Office
The Fellowship of the Ring (2001)	$125 million	$90.3 million	$968.7 million	$317.6 million

Source: pro.imdb.com.

The Lord of the Rings started the trend of fan interaction and fan management in the digital age. They incorporated the fandom, controlled the release of information to trusted members of their most active audience, and projected a positive, fan-like persona instilling confidence and trust in the fans for the film-makers and their processes. Many films such as *Eragon* (Stefen Fangmeier, 2007), *The Seeker: The Dark is Rising* (David L. Cunningham, 2007) and *The Golden Compass* (Chris Weitz, 2007) did not follow this path of fan interaction and involvement, and their US box office results pale in comparison to *The Lord of the Rings* and other event-film adaptation goliaths such as *Harry Potter*, *Twilight*, *The Hunger Games* and *Divergent*, who did work with their fans. These four films are just a small example of films produced after *The Lord of the Rings* which utilized their fan bases and presented their love of the texts and their appreciation of the process to the fans, which helped to retain their fan-based audience throughout production. From the initial pre-production considerations, to the filming and throughout the marketing leading up to the film, their practices ultimately led to significant box office returns after the films' releases, suggesting the film-makers of *The Lord of the Rings* had a good fan interaction practice: one franchise to teach them all. ●

GO FURTHER

Books

Studying the Event Film: 'The Lord of the Rings'
Harriet Margolis, Sean Cubitt, Barry King and Theirry Jutel (eds)

(Manchester: MUP, 2008)
Fans, Bloggers, and Gamers: Essays on Participatory Culture
Henry Jenkins
(New York: NYUP, 2006)

The Rough Guide to 'The Lord of the Rings'
Paul Simpson, Helen Rodiss and Michaela Bushell (eds)
(London: Haymarket, 2003)

'The Lord of the Rings': Official Movie Guide
Brian Sibley
(Boston, MA: Houghton Mifflin, 2001)

Sound Theory/Sound Practice (2nd edn)
Rick Altman
(London: Routledge, 1992)

Extras/Essays/Articles

'Post-classical fantasy cinema: *The Lord of the Rings*'
I. Q. Hunter
In Deborah Cartmell and Imelda Whelehan (eds). *The Cambridge Companion to Literature on Screen* (Cambridge: CUP, 2007), pp.154–66.

Online

'A Conversation with Rick Porras, part 1'
Kristin Thompson
The Frodo Franchise: 'The Lord of the Rings' and Modern Hollywood. 20 November 2007, www.kristinthompson.net/blog/?p=146.

'Ian McKellen's *Lord of the Rings* Pages'
Ian McKellen
McKellen.com. October 2001, http://www.mckellen.com/cinema/lotr/index.htm.

'Reactions to *Lord of the Rings: Fellowship of the Rings*.' *Pinoy Exchange.com*, 21 December 2001, http://www.pinoyexchange.com/forums/showthread.php?t=74048&page=3.

'Gordom Paddison: New Line Cinema'
Kathy McDonald
Variety. 1 August 2000, http://www.variety.com/article/VR1117784472.

Chapter
03

Reforging the Rings: Fan Edits and the Cinematic Middle-earth

Joshua Wille

→ In a video interview for the extended edition of The Two Towers (2003), author Brian Sibley recalls that

> There was a conversation that took place between [J. R. R.] Tolkien and C. S. Lewis, the creator of *The Chronicles of Narnia*, in which they were talking about the fact that they felt a frustration that they couldn't pick up and read the kind of books and stories that they liked to read, and they both came to this conclusion that, in the end, maybe they had to write the books they wanted to read.

A similar case for creative impulses could be made about contemporary fans who create alternative versions of feature films known as fan edits. Whereas Tolkien and Lewis composed their fantastic worlds by hand or through mechanical typewriters, fan editors today can use nonlinear digital video editing software to express their creative visions by re-editing scenes, replacing music and adding new material, among other techniques. As Jack Balkin observes in the essay, 'How Rights Change: Freedom of Speech in the Digital Era' (2004), a fan edit 'exemplifies what the new digital technologies make possible: ordinary people using these technologies to comment on, annotate, and appropriate mass media products for their own purposes and uses' (9–10). Fan edits are individual artistic expressions, articulations of personal readings and a means for fans to manifest the movies they want to see. For many *Lord of the Rings* enthusiasts, the expanding field of fan editing provides appealing reinterpretations of a film series that epitomize a revisionist mode in contemporary cinema.

Concerning fan editors

Fans have long enjoyed the freedom to experiment with cinematic media: in the 1970s and 1980s, there were fans that created their own abridged and alternative versions of films and television series by recording from one VCR to another, and before that era there were others who recut 8mm and 16mm film prints or recombined images in slide projectors in order to modify narratives and redefine character relationships. These practices can be understood as the antecedents of contemporary fan editing.

George Lucas can be credited with inspiring the current wave of fan editing primarily because he has led by example. Upon the release of his extensively revised versions of the *Star Wars* films in 1997, Lucas rationalized his changes in an interview with Ron Magid for *American Cinematographer*, claiming that 'Films never get finished, they get abandoned' (70). Five years later, Peter Rojas observed in *The Guardian* that alternative film versions such as the *Star Wars* special editions

> demolished the idea of a film as a single, finished product in the minds of the movie-viewing public. Instead we are headed towards a new conceptualization of a film as a permanent work-in-progress, which exists in multiple permutations, and can always be tinkered with in the future, whether by the director or by anybody else.

No history of fan editing can disregard the influence of Mike J. Nichols's *The Phantom Edit* (2000), a seminal fan edit based on *Star Wars Episode I: The Phantom Menace* (George Lucas, 1999) that was created on a personal computer and shared widely among *Star Wars* fans on peer-to-peer filesharing networks and in newsgroups. Instead of remaining underground like most earlier fan edits, *The Phantom Edit* achieved unprecedented popularity at a time when film revisionism was permeating Hollywood commercial products.

Reforging the Rings: Fan Edits and the Cinematic Middle-earth
Joshua Wille

In 'Fan Edits and the Legacy of *The Phantom Edit*' (2014), an essay on the history, theory and practice of fan editing, I explain that fan edits are unsanctioned alternative versions of feature films and television series that have been largely misunderstood 'as the work of disgruntled fans seeking to redeem the work of indifferent Hollywood magnates such as George Lucas' (23). Instead, I argue for a greater appreciation of the creative nature of fan edits. Unlike officially recognized film restorations or commercialized alternative cuts produced by Hollywood professionals, fan edits are noncommercial projects made by amateurs who skilfully wield contemporary consumer technology that was once exclusive to the media industry. Using desktop software, fan editors rip digital content from DVDs and Blu-ray discs and creatively reconfigure the material from one or more sources. In theory, fan editors are experimental film-makers whose work can be compared to music remixers because they create alternative versions of existing texts; in practice, fan editors are independent media artists and preservationists who share their work online with like-minded fans and curious viewers. Fan edits stand in the crossfire of ongoing debates on copyright, piracy and authorship, but they also contribute to an emerging creative discourse between fans and film producers in an era increasingly defined by revision.

Peter Jackson's acclaimed *The Lord of the Rings* film series is an exemplary case of Hollywood revisionism because it is widely known that each film was released in theatrical and extended versions. On DVD and Blu-ray, these extended editions provide fans with a wealth of additional narrative content and are presented in handsome packaging that resembles weathered, leather-bound copies of Tolkien's books. In a 2008 interview with Jeremy Smith for *Ain't It Cool News*, Peter Jackson explained that he does not consider the extended editions to be the definitive 'director's cuts' of his films because he recognizes value in both versions. While it is true that many Tolkien aficionados celebrated the production in Jackson's trilogy, they also criticized various incongruities with the original books, such as Gimli's comical behaviour and the presence of elves at Helm's Deep in *The Two Towers*. Several of these issues were addressed in fan edits as early as *The Two Towers: The Purist Edit* (2003), which was derived from a bootleg copy of a DVD screener originally intended for film critics and industry insiders but not for the public. *The Two Towers: The Purist Edit* was also not meant for commercial consumption, but it was essentially a speculative version of a film. Thus, the words 'FOR YOUR CONSIDERATION' conventionally superimposed on-screen in the DVD screener acquired new meaning when they were inherited by an anonymously produced revision: in the context of a fan edit, these words seemed to ask viewers to consider an alternative perspective on Peter Jackson's film as well as the avant-garde concept of fan editing. *The Two Towers: The Purist Edit* was among the first prominent edits to appear in the wake of *The Phantom Edit*, thereby encouraging wider audiences to consider the emergent work of fan editors.

Outsiders tend to spurn fan edits as illegal works because they are based on copyrighted material. However, like fan vidders and video essayists who remix digital content, fan editors often justify their work under the provisions of 'fair use' codified in section 107 of the United States Copyright Law, which permits the reproduction of copyrighted material for some noncommercial purposes, including criticism and commentary. The Digital Millennium Copyright Act (DMCA) in 1998 criminalized the circumvention of copy protection technology such as Digital Rights Management (DRM), but this has not stopped the production of these transformative works. Because it is often necessary to bypass DRM in order to create fanvids and fan edits, the Organization for Transformative Works has in recent years campaigned successfully for an exemption from the DMCA for such artworks with the Librarian of Congress. Moreover, the fan editing communities of *Fanedit.org* and *OriginalTrilogy.com* are outspoken opponents of media piracy and forbid the sale of fan edits, insisting that their creators and collectors purchase retail copies of fan edit source materials. Thus, *The Two Towers: The Purist Edit* and other fan edits derived from leaked DVD screeners are not recognized in *Fanedit.org*'s extensive Internet Fanedit Database.

None to rule them all

Audiences experience the *Lord of the Rings* films in multiple versions; the theatrical cuts have perhaps the broadest appeal because they contain the essential segments of the story, while the extended editions are ostensibly designed for fans that crave a more complete cinematic treatment of Tolkien's saga. Together, these two versions communicate to viewers that the *Lord of the Rings* film saga cannot be contained in a singular form. Far from the unrivalled quality of the One Ring in Tolkien's story, there is no definitive edition of the *Lord of the Rings* films 'to rule them all' but two equally valid commercial iterations available for consumption. Indeed, the *Lord of the Rings* films are representative of a broader trend in the film industry to release films deliberately in multiple cuts: an initial version is released to cinemas and marketed on home video, followed by 'director's cuts' or various alternative editions. Thus, popular films like those in the *Lord of the Rings* saga and the perennially revised *Star Wars* series are characterized by formal change. Fan edits diversify this model because they introduce more variation and represent new voices in a creative discourse surrounding revisionist cinema. Collectively, the existence of official and unofficial permutations of films increasingly demonstrate to contemporary audiences that cinema is a fluid art form rather than something commonly regarded as immutable or sacrosanct.

Fan editors generally strive for professionalism in their work with high-quality visuals and sound as well as seamless cuts. Thus, many of the narrative and aesthetic changes performed in *Lord of the Rings* fan edits are nuanced modifications that may be undetectable to viewers who are not informed of the specific revisions beforehand. *Lord of the Rings* fan edits often reshape Peter Jackson's films into closer approximations of the original novels, but fan editors acknowledge that adaptations necessarily make depar-

tures from their source material. For example, fan editors accept that Aragorn receives the sword Andúril prior to entering
the Path of the Dead in *The Return of the King* (2003) instead
of during his stay in Rivendell during *The Fellowship of the Ring* (2001). For the most
part, fan editors do not recut films heedlessly at the expense of narrative logic. Instead,
they compose annotated 'cut lists' that describe their motivation for each change in the
film and preview their works-in-progress to solicit advice and critiques in the fan editing
forums. Multiple fan edits based on the same film sometimes contain editorial patterns
that may reflect shared perspectives on plot and characters, but each fan edit has dis-
tinctive qualities. For fans of the *The Lord of the Rings*, each new permutation expands
the range of film versions available for exploration in the cinematic Middle-earth.

*Figure 1: Custom DVD box art
designed by CBB for The Lord
of the Rings: The Fellowship
of the Ring – Book Cut (HAL
9000 and Phil Dragash,
2009).*

Many paths to tread

The narrated prologue in Peter Jackson's *The Fellowship of the Ring* transports us to the
fictional world of Middle-earth, introducing the Rings of Power and the looming threat of
Sauron for uninitiated viewers. However, fan edits such as HAL 9000 and Phil Dragash's
The Lord of the Rings: The Fellowship of the Ring – Book Cut (2009) and Kerr's *The Lord
of the Rings: Book I – The Return of the Shadow* (2009) omit the prologue altogether
and open with Bilbo Baggins writing his memoir until his visitation from Gandalf. The effect of this simple cut is significant because removing the prologue permits the viewer
to gradually discover the truly dark nature of Bilbo's 'lucky ring' along with Gandalf and
Frodo through their actions. Alternatively, Spelledaren's *The Fellowship of the Ring: Remade* (2010) places less emphasis on Tolkien's original narrative and contains a modified version of the prologue in which Sauron does not explode with a shockwave when
defeated by Isildur.

Inspired by Tolkien's original six-book structure and suggested titles, Kerr's serial-
ized 'Red Book of Westmarch' fan edits are among the most narratively and aesthetically reverent versions of the *Lord of the Rings* films available. The final shot in each of
Kerr's installments dissolves to a stylized recreation of a printed page that announces
the conclusion of that particular book with an accompanying illustration, and his custom
designed DVDs include animated menus that visually trace the path of the characters
upon an aged map of Middle-earth. Much like the expansive Appendices in Tolkien's
books, Kerr's fan edits also include supplemental short subject films that elaborate on
the core narrative. For example, *The Return of the Shadow* contains 'The Finding of the
Ring', a seven-minute short that recounts Bilbo's first discovery of the One Ring through
a combination of animated visuals from the Jules Bass and Arthur Rankin Jr. adaptation of *The Hobbit* (1977) and narration from the *Lord of the Rings* audiobooks as read by
Robert Inglis (1991). Likewise, Kerr's *The Lord of the Rings: Book VI – The End of the Third
Age* (2010) includes 'The Tale of Aragorn and Arwen', a seventeen-minute short culled
from deleted material that depicts Aragorn and Arwen's romantic dilemma throughout

Figure 2: The title screen
from 'The Finding of the
Ring', included in the DVD for
The Lord of the Rings: Book
I – The Return of the Shadow
(Kerr, 2009).

Figure 3: The title screen
from 'The Tale of Aragorn
and Arwen', included in the
DVD for The Lord of the Rings:
Book VI – The End of the Third
Age (Kerr, 2010).

the *Lord of the Rings* saga.

For his first installment of *The Two Towers*, Kerr's *The Lord of the Rings: Book III – The Treason of Isengard* (2009) begins with the death of Boromir at Amon Hen and excludes all filmed scenes of Frodo and Sam. Instead, *The Treason of Isengard* chronicles the adventures of Merry, Pippin, Aragorn, Legolas and Gimli through Fangorn Forrest, and the lands of Rohan and Isengard, all based on the narrative progression in Tolkien's writing. *The Treason of Isengard* reflects many changes that other fans have attempted for *The Two Towers*, such as reducing comical moments with Gimli, omitting the warg attack and Aragorn's near-death experience, as well as removing the controversial appearance of Haldir and the elves at Helm's Deep. However, elves appear at Helm's Deep in Geminigod's *The Lord of the Rings: The Two Towers Rebuilt* (2012), which was partly inspired by the Tolkien books but conceived as more of a companion piece for Jackson's other films in the trilogy.

Kerr's *The Lord of the Rings: Book IV – The Journey of the Ringbearers* (2009) recombines material from *The Two Towers* and *The Return of the King* and focuses exclusively on the tribulations of Frodo and Sam as they make their way into Mordor with Gollum. By presenting different storylines from *The Two Towers* in separate feature films, Kerr engenders a greater appreciation of the passage of time and the geographical distance between the characters, thus undoing some of the narrative compression in Jackson's original film and sustaining our empathy for Frodo's arduous passage into Mordor. Both *The Journey of the Ringbearers* and HAL 9000's *The Lord of the Rings: The Two Towers: Sharkey's Purist Edition* (2009) cleverly intercut Frodo's conversation with Gollum in the Dead Marshes with a flashback to Smeagol's first encounter with the One Ring from *The Return of the King*. These fan edits, as well as Mukankakuna's *Lord of the Rings: The Two Towers Feanor Edition* (2012), eliminate Faramir's journey to Osgiliath with the ringbearers, while Geminigod's less reverent *The Two Towers Rebuilt* includes a modified version of the Osgiliath sequence in which Frodo does not attempt to give away the One Ring. These changes generally diminish the role of Faramir and refocus the narrative on Frodo's increasing corruption, but the degrees of their variation illustrate how fan editors creatively negotiate their own balances between reverence to Tolkien's original text and the idiosyncrasies of Peter Jackson's film adaptation.

For example, in Jackson's film of *The Return of the King*, the fight inside Shelob's lair seemed out of place to many Tolkien aficionados because the sequence originally appeared in the book *The Two Towers*. Instead of repositioning Shelob's appearance, HAL 9000's *The Lord of the Rings: The Return of the King: Sharkey's Purist Edition* (2010) and Mukankakuna's *The Lord of the Rings: The Return of the King Feanor Edition* (2012)

Reforging the Rings: Fan Edits and the Cinematic Middle-earth
Joshua Wille

Figure 4: Aragorn challenges Sauron while using the palantir at Minas Tirith in the extended edition of The Lord of the Rings: The Return of the King © New Line Cinema, 2003.

Figure 5: In a sequence from Battleship Isildur (Shannon Brownlee, 2013), Denethor feasts during the massacre but the bloodshed rattles the insurgent orcs

maintain this particular incongruity because they generally preserve the three-film structure of Jackson's adaptations. On the contrary, Kerr's *The Journey of the Ringbearers* concludes with Shelob's attack and Frodo's capture by the orcs, thus approximating Shelob's appearance in Tolkien's original *The Two Towers*.

Although most *Lord of the Rings* fan edits are attempts to reach a closer approximation of Tolkien's writing on the screen or to refine the narrative according to personal taste, there are others that take more unorthodox approaches. Stonehenge's *The Fellowship's Musical Journey* (2009) highlights the sounds of Middle-earth in *The Fellowship of the Ring* by removing most instances of dialogue and allowing sound effects to interplay with Howard Shore's evocative music score. Stonehenge's edit, like ADigitalMan's treatment of John Williams' score in *Star Wars: A Musical Journey* (2005), is reminiscent of some commercial DVDs and Blu-ray discs that provide a music-only audio track in order to highlight the work of the film composer. Shannon Brownlee's *Battleship Isildur* (2013) is a fan edit that combines material from the *Lord of the Rings* films and *Battleship Potemkin* (Sergei Eisenstein, 1925) in order to reinterpret their social context. Through a juxtaposition of shots, the combination of multiple elements on-screen and the creation of descriptive intertitles in Russian Cyrillic lettering, *Battleship Isildur* recasts the foul orcs from *The Lord of the Rings* as an oppressed, labouring underclass who rise against their cruel master, Saruman, and rescue innocent people from a brutal military ambush on the Potemkin Stairs.

Fans go ever ever on
Although the preceding selection of fan edits is by no means exhaustive, it does represent a remarkable body of creative work by *Lord of the Rings* fans. Several of these are efforts to conform Peter Jackson's film adaptations to the original *Lord of the Rings* narrative, but they are not merely the products of disgruntled fans. Reforged from existing media, these fan edits are better understood as remixes driven by individual readings of the cinematic Middle-earth. In their audio commentary for the *The Two Towers* extended edition, film-makers Peter Jackson, Fran Walsh and Philippa Boyens briefly discuss the possibility of making a chronological re-edit of the *Lord of the Rings* films. During this exchange, Jackson admits, 'I mean, well, people could do that with their – I shouldn't suggest this – you could do this with the sort of editing software on home computers these days. It's something that any fan could do,' to which Boyens suggests, 'Maybe they could do it for us and then we wouldn't need to do it ourselves.' Comments like these from the producers of the *Lord of the Rings* films add credence to the work of fan editors during a time when extended editions and director's cuts increasingly define film

culture. Computer technology has enabled *Lord of the Rings* fans to respond in kind, and like Tolkien's stories, fan editors demonstrate that unlikely characters can become agents of great change. ●

~~~~~~~~~~

GO FURTHER

Extracts/Essays/Articles

'Fan Edits and the Legacy of *The Phantom Edit*'
Joshua Wille
In *Transformative Works and Cultures*. 17 (2014) [Online], http://dx.doi.org/10.3983/twc.2014.0575

'How Rights Change: Freedom of Speech in the Digital Era'
Jack Balkin
In *Sydney Law Review*. 26: 1 (2004) [Online], http://digitalcommons.law.yale.edu/fss_papers/242/.

'An Expanded Universe'
Ron Magid
In *American Cinematographer*. 78: 2 (1997), pp. 60–70.

Online

'Mr Beaks Interviews Peter "Derek" Jackson about LOTR, KING KONG and Footwear!'
Jeremy Smith
Ain't It Cool News. 11 September 2008, http://www.aintitcool.com/node/16688.

'Hollywood: The People's Cut'
Peter Rojas
The Guardian. 25 July 2002, http://www.guardian.co.uk/film/2002/jul/25/internet.technology/.

Websites

Internet Fanedit Database, www.fanedit.org/ifdb

Fanedit.org, www.fanedit.org

Reforging the Rings: Fan Edits and the Cinematic Middle-earth
Joshua Wille

OriginalTrilogy.com, www.originaltrilogy.com

Fanedits.com, www.originaltrilogy.com/fan-edits

Films

The Lord of the Rings: The Return of the King, Peter Jackson, dir. (Los Angeles, CA: New Line Cinema, 2003).

The Lord of the Rings: The Two Towers, Peter Jackson, dir. (Los Angeles, CA: New Line Cinema, 2002). Extended Edition DVD (Los Angeles, CA: New Line Cinema, 2003).

The Lord of the Rings: The Fellowship of the Ring, Peter Jackson, dir. (Los Angeles, CA: New Line Cinema, 2001).

Fan edits

Battleship Isildur, Shannon Brownlee (2013).

Lord of the Rings: The Return of the King Feanor Edition, Mukankakuna (2012).

Lord of the Rings: The Two Towers Feanor Edition, Mukankakuna (2012).

The Lord of the Rings: The Two Towers Rebuilt, Geminigod (2012).

The Lord of the Rings: Book V – The War of the Ring, Kerr (2010).

The Lord of the Rings: Book VI – The End of the Third Age, Kerr (2010).

The Fellowship of the Ring: Remade, Spelledaren (2010).

The Lord of the Rings: The Return of the King: Sharkey's Purist Edition, HAL 9000 (2010).

The Fellowship's Musical Journey, Stonehenge (2009).
The Lord of the Rings: Book I – The Return of the Shadow, Kerr (2009).

The Lord of the Rings: Book II – The Ring Goes South, Kerr (2009).

The Lord of the Rings: Book III – The Treason of Isengard, Kerr (2009).

The Lord of the Rings: Book IV – The Journey of the Ringbearers, Kerr (2009).

The Lord of the Rings: The Fellowship of the Ring: Sharkey's Purist Edition, HAL 9000 (2009).

The Lord of the Rings: The Fellowship of the Ring – Book Cut, HAL 9000 and Phil Dragash (2009).

The Lord of the Rings: The Two Towers: Sharkey's Purist Edition, HAL 9000 (2009).

The Two Towers: The Purist Edit (2003).

Chapter
04

Walking Between Two Lands, or How Double Canon Works in The Lord of the Rings Fan Films

Miguel Ángel Pérez-Gómez

→ Fan films as fandom practice are common since the arrival of the Star Trek community consolidated media fandom in the mid-1970s. However, it was not until 1998 that a fan film entitled Troops (Kevin Rubio), inspired by George Lucas's Star Wars universe, boosted this phenomenon. Thus, the production of fan films has become what we now consider as a stable custom among fans of any kind of text.

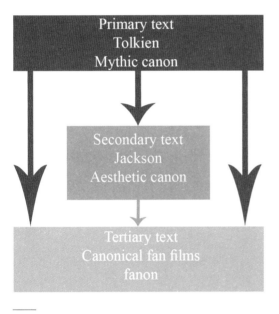

Figure 1: LOTR three-level text canon.

Nevertheless, in the case of *The Lord of the Rings* (*LOTR*), this practice became usual after the release of the trilogy directed by Peter Jackson. What makes this case paradigmatic is that before the films there was a well-established and organized fandom around Tolkien's universe. Even though the work of the English author establishes a clear world canon, only the release of Jackson's films established a canonical aesthetics that was assumed by fan creators.

Thus, fan films made by fans of Middle-earth use these two canons to create their productions: on the one hand, the fictional universe set up by Tolkien; on the other hand, the aesthetics imposed by Peter Jackson. So much so that those fan films which can be considered 'serious' – in other words, those that try to 'fit' into this universe – just choose the visual canon designed by the New Zealand director, but try to fill those gaps left in the films. This chapter shows how fans use the literary and cinematic texts to build a convergent discourse in which secondary characters and situations that had been dealt with tangentially become important in a clear effort to be a part of the canonical filmic chronology of Middle-earth one way or another.

Double canon and the formation of tertiary texts

Canonical or serious fan films are those whose main goal is to fit in the canonical chronology. As a general rule, the production of these contents has its origin in what we consider the primary texts. For John Fiske the texts relate to each other as: primary, secondary and tertiary texts. Applying that to *LOTR* we find a paradigmatic case within fandom's creative production, in which two texts of different levels are equally important for fan creators: in the primary text, Tolkien defines a mythical canon through the description of characters, anthropology, history, chronology, language and geography; while Peter Jackson's movies, as secondary texts, stay within the boundaries of Tolkien's literary world, at the same time, as Fleischhack says, they are strongly marked and influenced by Alan Lee and John Howe's artwork, definitively creating an aesthetic canon; the tertiary text is the end of text circulation where the two canons converge with a clear aim to create a single discourse.

Peter Jackson's trilogy gathers up the aspects through which Tolkien defines his mythical canon, but the facts found in the English author's narratives are reworked by Jackson into an aesthetical product openly oriented toward the epic. To this we must

Walking Between Two Lands, or How Double Canon Works in The Lord of the Rings Fan Films
Miguel Ángel Pérez-Gómez

add: the thematic use of colour (filters); the thematic centrality of the Ring; the sense of epic shown through long shots increased by Jackson's tendency to excess; overuse of high- and low-angle shots, as well as Dutch angles; and asynchronous editing. All these resources appear in an atavistic and repetitive way in fan films.

The cult text as a starting point for tertiary texts

Both the literary and the film trilogies are indisputably cult pieces that have reached the same level at generating a response and an active audience. Umberto Eco considers that cult texts must promote 'cyclic return' in the sense that the audience return to them again and again despite already knowing their plot, their outcome and their quality. This phenomenon establishes a link between the audience and the texts. For the Italian scholar a cult text uses what he calls eternal archetypes, situations that have presided over stories of all time including historical and contemporary myths. 'Because it is vaguely perceived that clichés talk to each other and celebrate a reunion party', i.e. a cult text must be fully 'furnished', be 'dismountable' and be a 'text of texts' (see Eco) It is a series of elements that lead to fascination, making a text a 'phenomenon worthy, but something else of worship', that is: of cult.

To Hills, cult texts must have characteristics that distinguish them: authorship, endlessly deferred narrative and the creation of a vast narrative space (the so-called hyperdiegesis), of which only a small part is shown. The hyperdiegesis combines with what Dolezel termed 'gap/fact': the gap is what the story omits, whereas the fact is what the story does explain, that is, the canon. Pugh defines the latter as 'the source of material accepted as authentic and, within the fandom, known by all readers in the same way that myth and folk-tale were once commonly known' (41). Conversely, a gap is what is omitted or not narrated in the text, and can give rise to creative productions through which fans attempt to become part of the filmic canon in one way or another, at least in the *LOTR* case.

LOTR fan films double canon

We can consider the fans of Peter Jackson's films as second-generation fans, understood not in a chronological sense, but with regard to the relationship with the text toward which they feel affection. Firstly they know the secondary text, or at least this is the one used as a reference, but afterwards they turn their interest to Tolkien's work. We must consider this kind of fan not only as a viewer who has a great knowledge about the movies and the books, but also as an individual who establishes a conversation with the text. Thus, the film fan feels an urge to narratively expand the film trilogy by filling its gaps with facts from the books, or less frequently with audio-visual pieces that are not reflected in either the films or the written works.

In accordance with Wolf's typology we can divide these fan films in relation to the film canon, as interventions relative to the original text, into five major groups: the sequels, the prequels, the midquels, the transquels and the paraquels. Wolf contends that the sequel 'takes place after an existing story, usually shares some common elements with the original story it follows, carrying them forward in time' (205) . By contrast the prequel is 'a story that comes before an existing story and acts as an expanded backstory […] and the final ending state is more than predictable' (205). Pugh considers that 'only closed canons can have sequels, as such. But prequels can happen in any universe' (26).

To Wolf, midquels are those 'works which come in between already-existing story materials', the so called *missing scenes*; Pugh defines it as the 'incidents, conversations, interactions, that take place within the timescale of canon' (26). These are actions that may have occurred but have not been shown explicitly. Within this category there are two distinct types: interquels and intraquels. An 'interquel is a sequence element that occurs between existing works in a series, whereas an intraquel is a sequence element that occurs during a gap within a single existing work'. These are exercises of direct intervention into the primary texts, but other categories widen them: the transquels 'are broad in scope, giving historical context to the works they encompass' (Wolf 209); and the paraquels show events 'from other perspectives of different characters, the paraquel is an entire work covering the same events or period in time from a different perspective' (Wolf 210).

These are the categories under which we can situate those serious fan films created in reference to that double canon. Each has an immediate relation to the cinematic work, because of the aesthetics and visual storytelling influence, and secondly with the literary.

Sequels

Canonical sequels are productions that touch plots belonging to literary canon tangentially, so they can be considered as pure fantasies or speculations by fans. The first example is *The Sons of Elrond* (Toby and Cody McClure, 2008), an animated short film that takes place in the Fourth Age of Middle-earth and is led by the sons of Elrond travelling to the Forest of Lorien to relive old battles of the past.

The Age of Men (Nikolai Monson, 2006) takes place 100 years after the War of the Ring, and its main characters are Aragorn's grandchildren. They receive news about Sauron's rebirth and his search of a second ring of power lost in a battlefield. One of the brothers finds it and suffers the same consequences as those who have possessed the Ring before. The plot of this amateur production is minimal and its 77 minutes are devoted largely to battles between humans and orcs. These fights are what we consider as fanon, a constant in *LOTR* fan films.

Another example is *The Fourth Age* (Lyn, 2013), a short film with no plot and poor execution in which a group of children accompanied by an adult woman flee from orcs. Only a mention of Aragorn's children at one point, along with the title, links it to the double canon. On the other hand, *Broken Bow* (Sam Hawkeye, 2013), a teaser trailer of a

Walking Between Two Lands, or How Double Canon Works in The Lord of the Rings Fan Films
Miguel Ángel Pérez-Gómez

future fan film that takes place in the years of Aragorn's reign, explains how the Rangers are trying to rescue one of their members that has been kidnapped during a conflict with the Easterlings.

Figure 2: Halbaron (Howard Corlett) in Born of Hope © 2009, Actors at Work

    Trailers for fan films that have not been finished or that have not even gone beyond the project-stage usually go unnoticed, since some fan films are themselves trailers. Such is the case of the former example, which in this format becomes unexpectedly the final product. The same happens with *The Palantir* (Unknown, 2010), another teaser trailer for a fan film that can be located within this category. Other fan films remain unfinished or lost, as is the case of *La Guerra de la ira/The War of Rage* (Unknown, 2002), a movie that was made in Spain, and about which there is no information other than some news and photos of the shooting. This piece takes place in the time of Aragorn and Arwen's grandchildren at the beginning of the Fourth Age, when a great plague is devastating Middle-earth. These fan films share a number of characteristic features: using a timeline based on the Tolkien canon; adopting Peter Jackson's film aesthetics; and referring to the facts and characters in the movies to benefit from their popularity.

Prequels
To Wolf, prequels 'rely on the audience knowledge' but the most important thing is that these productions try to contribute a new starting point for the narrative (265). In the first two cases, we shall see how both fan films are unequivocally linked to the Tolkien canon and aesthetically inspired by Jackson's films. Regarding the latter there are similarities in the credits and the music, which was created expressly for these productions but bears a strong resemblance to the original soundtrack Howard Shore

Figure 3: Goblok (Gareth Brough) in The Hunt for Gollum © 2009, Independent Online Cinema.

composed for the film trilogy.

The first of these films is *Born of Hope* (Kate Madison, 2009) based on Appendix A dedicated to the 'Annals of the Kings and Rulers', in the section dedicated to 'The Númenórean Kings'. The plot takes place at the end of the Third Age of Middle-earth, when Sauron's power is increasing, and the orcs under his command are engaged in chasing the few remaining members of Elendil the Highlineage, who are heirs to the Dúnedain. The film depicts how Sauron searches for the Ring through his horde of orcs, and the vicissitudes of the Dúnedain as they defend themselves against their attacks. The interest of this fan film also lies in seeing the relationship between Gilran and Arathorn, Aragorn's parents. *Born of Hope* gives as much importance to the literary canon as to the cinematic canon, focusing on the search for the Ring. Aesthetically, it follows Jackson's proposals: a dull, sad, greyish palette of colours; the use of large panoramic shots and Dutch angles; and, above all, the slow motion in violent action scenes with a cathartic intention.

At first glance *The Hunt for Gollum* (Chris Bouchard, 2009) should be a *missing scene*, as it pertains to events described in the book but not depicted in the film. The story is set seventeen years before *The Fellowship of the Ring*; however, this fan film is narratively constructed as a prequel when Gandalf fears that Gollum may reveal the location of the Ring to Sauron, so the wizard sends Aragorn on his quest. In this production the figure of Gollum helps us to see how canon becomes fanon, in this case the verification of a trend. The description of the creature that appears in *The Hobbit* is as follows: 'He was Gollum – as dark as darkness, except for two big round pale eyes in his thin face' (67). However, Jackson ignores the physical darkness of the character

Walking Between Two Lands, or How Double Canon Works in The Lord of the Rings Fan Films
Miguel Ángel Pérez-Gómez

Figure 4: Promotional image from Halifirien © 2009, Tom Robinson Productions.

prioritizing the round face and the very bright, expressive eyes inspired by Alan Lee's illustrations for some of Tolkien's stories.

Another fan-film that can be placed in this segment dedicated to prequels is *Diari dalla Terza Era/Diary of the Third Age* (Claudio Ripalti, 2013), a short film that explains the clash between a knight and the Witch-King of Angmar, the latter characterized as a Nazgul as it appears in Jackson's film. Finally, the knight is killed by the necromancer. Despite temporal distance, the fan film narrative retains the geographical and aesthetical canon. In the cases of these prequels, at least in the first two examples, we have a couple of productions seeking – largely by the high values of production – to fit within the film trilogy by explaining elements absent from it.

Midquels, transquels and paraquels

Midquels have two variants: interquels and intraquels (in this case there's only examples of the latter). The first one is *Halifirien* (Tom Robinson, 2009), whose story develops within the third film when the beacons of Gondor must be lighted to help the Kingdom of Rohan. This fan film takes place in Halifirien, a mountain belonging to Tolkien's imaginary geographical universe that appears in *Unfinished Tales* (1980). The Halifirien is an important peak of the Ered Nimrais, on top of which is located the last beacon of Gondor's Kingdom. The story has a very basic premise: the protagonists are two brothers whose mission is to light the last beacon between the two kingdoms during the siege of the troops of Sauron at Minas Tirith. Notwithstanding the task is not easy they will have to fight the hordes of orcs again and again, occupying much of the footage, leading to the epic of blood and skirmishes with orcs to exhaustion. This narrative does not belong legitimately to this universe but the use of the geographical space defined in the fan film spatially places it in this world. Jackson's aesthetics are less evident because of the amateur values of production.

Another case of intraquel is *The Road to the End* (Jason Wright, 2012), a serious attempt in which there are only two characters: Frodo and Gollum. While the actor who plays Frodo is characterized as in the movies, the actor in the role of Gollum is a young boy dressed in sportswear. This production revolves around Frodo trying to learn more about Gollum's psychology, while this creature's dual personality starts making plans of his own. These intraquels or missing scenes work because of the consistency of the films and their iconic value; however, their length should be limited to short pieces (vignettes) that explain what happens along temporal ellipses, in this case, the lighting of the beacons and a fragment of Frodo and Gollum's journey.

The particularity of transquels is that they have a limited focused narrative seeking to help understand the context or a certain historical aspect. In the case of the universe created by Tolkien can be found fan documentaries in short format attempting to address a specific topic. Usually the material used is stock images, extracted frames from movies, video games, picture books, RPGs, etc.

A couple of very specific cases that perfectly exemplify this trend are *The Gods of Middle Earth Documentary* (Toca de Minas, 2012) and *Historia de Angmar/History of Angmar* (Tomba Millan, 2013), two pieces whose titles explain their contents and that they are still transversal to Tolkien's issues.

A paraquel is a way to re-explain the facts from another point of view, rewriting them or placing them in similar characters. As is the case of *The Peril to the Shire* (Douglas Dunklin, 2007), a three and a half-hour film in which we are told the adventures of hobbits who embark on a similar adventure as Frodo and company. These are Rose Cotton and her nephew Hamfoot, who make their way to Budgeford, but never reach their destination because on the way they meet a wounded elf. The maker of this fan film tries to explore a 'what if' scenario based on the Appendices, in a story that starts four months after Frodo and co. leave the Shire. *The Peril to the Shire* contains excerpts from Peter Jackson's movies and the soundtrack itself, and tries in a humble way to imitate the films' aesthetics, common topographic issues and use of geographical canon. This is a fan film made for fun and educational purposes, which is not available on the web in full but only as a trailer and some video fragments.

In conclusion, fan films based on the universe of *LOTR* have a split personality. On the one hand, they are based directly or indirectly on the primary text of Tolkien, but give centrality to the secondary text created by Peter Jackson. This is a kind of milestone in the fandom phenomenon because such productions are non-existent until the appearance of the film adaptations. It is one of the few occasions, if not the only one, of the phenomenon that the tertiary text has more in common with the secondary than the primary text. On the other hand, it is interesting to see how authorial features of the New Zealand director have become standard for amateur film-makers, transforming the aesthetic canon into fanon. ●

Walking Between Two Lands, or How Double Canon Works in The Lord of the Rings Fan Films
Miguel Ángel Pérez-Gómez

GO FURTHER

Books

Building Imaginary Worlds: The Theory and History of Subcreation
Mark J. P. Wolf
(London: Routledge, 2013)

The Lord of the Rings
J. R. R. Tolkien
(London: Harper Collins, 2007 [1954–55])

The Hobbit
J. R. R. Tolkien
(London, Harper Collins, 2006 [1937])

The Democratic Genre: Fan Fiction in a Literary Context
Sheenagh Pugh
(Dridgend: Poetry Wales Press Ltd., 2005)

Fan Cultures
Matt Hills
(London: Routledge, 2002)

Heterocosmica: Fiction and Possible Worlds
Lubomir Dolezel
(Baltimore: Johns Hopkins University Press, 2000)

Faith in Fakes: Travels in Hyperreality
Umberto Eco
(London: Vintage, 1995)

Unfinished Tales
J. R. R. Tolkien
(London: Harper Collins, [1980] 1992)

Extracts/Essays/Articles

'The Lord of the Fans: The Evolution of the *Lord of the Rings* Fandom'
Maria Fleischhack

In Dieter Petzold (ed.). *Inklings: Jahrbuch fur Literatur und Ästhetik. [Inklings: The Journal of Literature and Aesthetics]*
(Moers: Brendow, 2010), pp. 96–106.

'The Cultural Economy of Fandom'
John Fiske
In Lisa Lewis (ed.). *Adoring Audience: Fan Culture and Popular Media*
(London: Routledge, 1992), pp. 30–49.

Online

'De nuevo, La Guerra de la Ira.' *Elfenomeno.com*, 22 November 2002, http://www.elfenomeno.com/info/ver/8894/titulo/De-nuevo-La-Guerra-de-la-Ira.

'"The War of Rage" Fan Film'
Xoanon
TheOneRing.net. 1 December 2002, http://archives.theonering.net/perl/news-view/7/1038797438.

Films and Fan films

The Fourth Age, Lyn (USA: Kidorama Productions, 2013).

Broken Bow, Sam Hawkeye (Netherlands,2013).

Diari dalla Terza Era/Diary of the Third Age, Claudio Ripalti (Italy, 2013)

Historia de Angmar/History of Angmar, Tomba Millan (Spain: Tomba Millan, 2013).

The Road to the End, Jason Wright (Canada: New Loyalty Entertainment, 2012).

The Gods of Middle Earth Documentary, Toca de Minas (Brazil: Estadual do Conselho Branco Sociedade Tolkien, 2012).

The Palantir, Unknown (Unknown, 2010).

Born of Hope, Kate Madison (UK: Actors at Work, 2009).

The Hunt for Gollum, Chris Bouchard (UK: Independent Online Cinema, 2009).

Walking Between Two Lands, or How Double Canon Works in The Lord of the Rings Fan Films
Miguel Ángel Pérez-Gómez

Halifirien, Tom Robinson (Ireland: Tom Robinson Productions, 2009).

The Sons of Elrond, Toby and Cody McClure (USA: Seakings Creative Studios, 2008).

The Peril to the Shire, Douglas Dunklin (USA: Status Productions, 2007).

The Age of Men, Nikolai Monson (USA: 1409 Productions, 2006).

The Lord of the Rings: The Return of the King, Peter Jackson (New Zealand/USA: New Line Cinema, 2003).

The Lord of the Rings: The Two Towers, Peter Jackson (New Zealand/USA: New Line Cinema, 2002).

La Guerra de la ira/The War of Rage (Unknown, 2002)

The Lord of the Rings: The Fellowship of the Ring, Peter Jackson (New Zealand/USA: New Line Cinema, 2001)

"NEW ZEALAND IS NOT A SMALL COUNTRY, BUT A LARGE VILLAGE."

PETER JACKSON

Chapter
05

On Party Business: True-fan Celebrations in New Zealand's Middle-earth

Lorna Piatti-Farnell

→ Within the areas of fandom and tourism, a large amount of studies already exists on the reimagination of New Zealand as 'Middle-earth' and the consequences – positive and negative as they may be perceived – of this move. This reimagination has of course attracted the keen attention of the fans themselves, who, over the years, have hailed New Zealand as the perfect location for the filming of *The Lord of the Rings (LOTR)* trilogy, and praised Peter Jackson for his cinematic vision in capturing the beauty of the country in ways that Tolkien would have approved of.

A similar interest – although on a much smaller scale – has been found in exploring the establishment and success of *LOTR*-specific attractions such as Hobbiton Movie Set Tours: the park experience, located near the village of Mata Mata in the North Island of New Zealand, that transports visitors into the world of the Shire, complete with life-size hobbit holes (see Peaslee). A much smaller amount of literature, however, exists on the presentation of Hobbiton as not merely a *LOTR* attraction, but as a veritable 'fansite', and all that this connection entails. It is therefore important to address this gap. In response to this, this chapter enquires into the experience of Hobbiton as a 'fan-practice', and the social, cultural, and symbolic meanings associated with it. I place particular emphasis on the newly-emerged practice of 'parties in Hobbiton', where fans choose this location as a venue for their closest personal celebrations, from birthdays to weddings. In looking at this, I am particularly interested in exploring what brings 'fans' to invest in Hobbiton as a celebration backdrop, and what particular sense of both 'experience' and 'entitlement' is revealed by this choice.

The reimagining of the New Zealand landscape as 'Middle-earth', and the incredible economic and cultural successes for the country that have resulted from this move, point us in the direction of seeing this cinematic revision as part of a consumption system that goes beyond simple notions of film location, or even film tourism. Undoubtedly, the seemingly 'untouched' nature of the New Zealand landscape provided an appropriate canvas for the painting of hills and mountains as coming straight from Tolkien's imagination. Cynical reviewers of Jackson's film trilogy have often suggested that the landscape was the real 'star' of the films, while the acting left a lot to be desired. And there is no denying that the tourism industry of New Zealand capitalized on this connection, pushing for visiting the country's landscape as the only way to experience 'Middle-earth'. Several tourism websites even go as far as claiming that New Zealand is 'the home of Middle-earth' (see www.nzhomeofmiddleearth.com). Chris Rojek recently claimed that when discussing travel and tourism – especially film tourism – a certain 'mythical' reimagining is at work, and it is truly unavoidable (52). By 'mythical', Rojek intends the social visualization of a geographical location into a 'place', a category that is constructed only through an index of real and imagined references. As far as New Zealand/Middle-earth is concerned, this visualization, however, is more than simply an instance of ecotourism. With ecotourism, visitors are 'sold' by the idea of visiting untouched and pristine natural areas, often inaccessible to the general public. And while there is a certain desire to promote New Zealand as a 'pure' land to the tourist - see the famous '100% New Zealand Pure' adverts - there is something quite different at work with promoting the film locations for *The Lord of the Rings* as the only spot where one can really see Middle-earth (see www.newzealand.com). The very idea and existence of Hobbiton, with all its tempting options for 'experience', pays testament to this.

In the wake of *The Lord of the Rings* trilogy being completed and shown in cinemas, avid fans could already visit the hilly area of Mata Mata where the Hobbiton scenes had

On Party Business: True-fan Celebrations in New Zealand's Middle-earth
Lorna Piatti-Farnell

been filmed – which feature mainly in _The Fellowship of the Ring_ (2001) and _The Return of the King_ (2003). During this time, however, the experience was more akin to location spotting, rather than a tour of the set. One could only view the green hills and surrounding areas, with nothing but disappointing hints of where the hobbit holes had once stood, together with all their inevitable props and decorations. This, however, was not to last. As far as New Zealand was concerned, _LOTR_-location tours had already proven to be a successful activity for fans, and the launching of the _Hobbit_ trilogy renewed the interest in all things _LOTR_-related. It became clear that both avid fans and casual spectators had a distinct interest in viewing the actual set of the films, and craved to experience the 'feel' of the location as it is shown in the story. This had also been confirmed by other existing examples in the industry, ranging from historically successful ones – such as Universal Studios in California – to the Warner Bros. Studio Tour for Harry Potter in London, the latter offering a true-fan experience of the sets, complete with character evolution laboratories and, of course, plenty of photographic and merchandise-buying opportunities. So the idea of 'Hobbiton' as a permanent site evolved from a simple location tour to a real-set experience, able to immerse the fans into the world of _The Lord of the Rings_ in a clear and explicit way.

Hobbiton as a 'fansite'
As a real attraction and visitor park, Hobbiton opened its doors in 2011. It re-branded itself as Hobbiton Movie Set Tours, and developed on its promise to offer just that. It comes as no surprise to learn that the attraction has a great claim over its place in _The Lord of the Rings_ cinematic narrative; this is mirrored in one of the promotional slogans on its website, telling the fans that they can 'Discover the real Middle-Earth at the Hobbiton™ Movie Set' (www.hobbitontours.com). The geographical siting of Hobbiton was kept as Mata Mata, but the outlook and experience of the location completely changed to what fans can experience today upon visiting: hobbit holes are maintained in their full working order, just as they appear in the films, complete with everyday accessories such as food, dinner plates, and washing lines. The idea is to make visitors 'believe' that that they are just dropping by the village in the middle of an average day, and that the hobbits actually live there, and may have just popped out for a walk. This new set offers a very 'true' experience of Hobbiton, as if it were never a work of fiction, but an existing location, with real inhabitants. In addition, visitors can enjoy gazing upon a well-

Figure 2: A view of the Green Dragon in Hobbiton © 2015, Hobbiton Movie Set Tours

conceived working water mill and, arguably, the star of the Hobbiton experience: the Green Dragon, a fully-working pub – inspired by the establishment of the same name, as mentioned in both Jackson's trilogy and Tolkien's books – where visitors can stop for a glass of Hobbiton-brewed ale, or even a delicious scone. The Green Dragon is a faithful and quite stunning replica of the pub shown in the movies: every detail is carefully conceived, from the old-fashioned chairs to the fireplace – always live and crackling, even in the summer – and an impressive wooden carving of the 'green dragon' above the bar area. The Green Dragon aims at delivering a 'true life' experience to the visitors, and adds an even greater layer of authenticity to the fan experience of the site.

Indeed, the success of reimagining a simple slice of farmland in the North Island of New Zealand as 'Hobbiton' uncovers the impact of fandom in creating a sense of 'place' for the location which is governed by 'virtuality and simulation' (Tzanelli 22). More than any other *LOTR*-related location in New Zealand, Hobbiton reveals the extent to which the fans' own desire to visualize and experience the world of the films creates its own microcosm of metaphors, and connected consumption practices. The cinematic consumption patterns that have made the *LOTR* trilogy the success that it is rely on a multi-faceted and polymorphous milieu. The effective visualization of a location such as Hobbiton depends on the fan practices that, in turn, rely on the consumption of 'signs': it is not just what the location 'looks' like, but what it 'signifies'. Its meaning, however, is not intrinsic, it is given: to a general viewer, it is simply a careful construction of buildings and objects, used in the filming of the trilogy, as well as its *Hobbit* sequels, and perhaps preserved more as a form of museum than anything else. To a 'fan', however, the meaning of Hobbiton is revealed through what it represents: loyalty to a beloved franchise, as well as knowledge of its production and narrative intricacies. And, above all, Hobbiton condenses the 'fantasy of the fantasy' into a liveable experience: the desire to become part of the films' magical world is made accessible, even for just a short period of time. Jean Baudrillard would identify this attributed system of meaning as pivoting on the recognition of 'sign value': what an 'object' – concrete or ephemeral – 'means' to those who encounter it, and how that meaning is reliant on belief and shared vision (Baudrillard, 36).

There is no denying that the fans' interest in not only visiting Hobbiton, but also, as we will see, in hosting their personalized *LOTR*-themed party on site, is the result of an attachment that is figurative more than anything else. It might be useful to recall Pierre Bourdieu's suggestion here that all cultural production – from film to music, and cultural experiences like tours and even holidays – is based upon creations of meaning that are undoubtedly 'symbolic': Bourdieu defines 'symbolic capital' as 'charisma', and and almost 'magical power' that is accumulated through recognition and a shared and agreed sense of 'prestige' (2). Therefore, all cultural experiences – both concrete, like objects, or ephemeral, like movie-set tours – are reliant on the shared agreements

On Party Business: True-fan Celebrations in New Zealand's Middle-earth
Lorna Piatti-Farnell

of those who experience it – the fans, in the case of *LOTR* – in order to gain any value at all. That value lives in perception, but is, nonetheless, very actual in its presence. The value of any cultural production is variable and always contingent on the belief of those who encounter it. The perception of Hobbiton as 'important' – which is inevitably unconscious on the fans' part – bestows a higher value to the site of the movie set as unmissable. The Hobbiton experience, therefore, is afforded symbolic capital by the fans themselves, as it is projected both within and without as a treasured experience, and, perhaps, even the recognizable interest of a 'true fan'. Needless to say, symbolic capital also brings with it what Bourdieu calls 'economic capital': the commercial value that is attributed to the symbolic experience, and what the consumers will be willing to pay once they envisage the experience itself as 'significant'. The two forms of capital converge in the fan experience of Hobbiton, as the perception of the experience itself as 'important' will inevitably make the steep ticket price an obvious and just outcome of such a wonderful set-up.

Figure 3: Bilbo's 'hobbit hole' in Hobbiton, with the now famous sign of 'No Admittance. Except on Party Business' © 2015, Hobbiton Movie Set Tours.

Parties in Hobbiton

The most intricate, symbolic, fan-based function of Hobbiton, however, is not simply uncovered by considering the very act of visiting as a fan practice. Indeed, the real recognition of experience and value is to be found in the propensity for fans to host their own parties on site. The management of Hobbiton is very keen to advertise the fans' ability to hold their own personalized functions on the premises (see the 'Events and Functions' section at www.hobbitontours.com). The location's website proudly declares that guests can hold their parties in multiple areas of the park: they can host a personalized dinner at the Green Dragon, where everything, from the food to the table decor, will be taylored to their needs, giving them an 'authentic' experience of the hobbits' pub; or, the guests can host their wedding in an especially set up marquee that will be fully decorated and accessorized to recall the infamous 'Hobbiton celebrations', as seen in *The Lord of the Rings* trilogy.

If interested, the avid guests can even request the presence of musicians who will be appropriately dressed in film-related costumes, complete with elven and hobbit pointy ears. Undoubtedly, once the location is transformed to meet the needs of the personalized party, it 'looks' and 'feels' rather spectacular, and truly worthy of the money that guests lavish on the experience.

One might be tempted to suggest that the public just 'like' Hobbiton as a location for their parties and celebrations, but this would not be a satisfying answer. Any preference is suffused with cultural practices, and even the simple fact of 'liking' a location carries with it implications of a cultural nature. The main question here being, would anyone who is not a 'true fan' of *LOTR* even consider hosting an important celebration in Hobbiton? The answer to this would most likely be, probably not. Nonetheless, one needs to go beyond this simple reaction, steeped as it is in the dangers of common sense, and enquire into the nature of that decision, and the grounds for such an inclination.

The decision to have a *LOTR*-themed party in Hobbiton, especially if it is an 'important' one such as a wedding, signals that the enjoyment and pleasure that fans derive from engaging with the beloved trilogy surpasses any notion of a passive process of consumption: it is more than mere reception, it is a form of performance (see Duffett). As far as the world of *The Lord of the Rings* is concerned, the transformation of 'fiction' into 'real life', as enacted by the fandom, is a carefully arranged interplay of appropriation, objectification, re-enactment, and ownership. Being part of the world of Middle-earth is an opportunity seemingly afforded by immersing instances of everyday life into the imaginary world of the film in Hobbiton, and involves the fan becoming an 'active' agent in not only suspending disbelief – this is really Hobbiton, this is really Middle-earth – but also in constructing layers of meaning that are cited in both symbolic attribution and participation.

In a number of *LOTR*-themed parties, especially weddings, participants often indulge in wearing clothes that resemble the costumes worn by the characters in the films. Unsurprisingly, a romantic set-up of choice is that which resembles the emotional moment when Aragorn (Viggo Mortensen) and Arwen (Liv Tyler) are reunited and officially 'promised' to each other at the end of *The Return of the King*. One need only enter keywords such as 'Lord of the Rings Wedding' into an online search engine to be immediately presented with the astonishing reality that many a groom have chosen to don the surcoat tunic embroidered with the White Tree of Gondor, as worn by Aragorn himself in the movies; similarly, many brides have chosen to walk down the aisle in an Elvish gown – distinctly medieval in its sartorial style – complete with Elvish-like jewellery, in an effort to look just like Arwen. Even such a rudimentary, non-scientific method reveals the influence that *The Lord of the Rings* has had on spectators, and the ways in which the outlook and experience of the films have impacted the ways of being and lifestyle of the fandom.

Naturally, not all *LOTR*-themed weddings – or even general parties – have taken place in the movies' locations in New Zealand. Similarly, not all brides and grooms have decided to wear clothes that recall the attire of Aragorn and Arwen, even if they are

On Party Business: True-fan Celebrations in New Zealand's Middle-earth
Lorna Piatti-Farnell

Figure 4: The interior of the Green Dragon, set up for a private party © 2015, Hobbiton Movie Set Tours.

having a *LOTR*-themed wedding in every other way, from venue decoration to invitations and party favours. The same can be said for other forms of celebrations that have gathered inspiration from the trilogy, and uncountable examples from this category can be found by quickly searching on the Internet. Nonetheless, the fans' assiduous desire to replicate the authentic outlook of the trilogy, complete with clothing and set-up, becomes even more enhanced and explicit once the wedding celebrations are transported – physically and metaphorically – to the movie set of Hobbiton. Undeniably, having a *LOTR*-themed wedding in Hobbiton adds both magic and tangibility to the experience, and makes it feel more 'real' to those who experience it.

This intent of resembling the favourite characters from the trilogy could be viewed as a form of impersonation. Generally speaking, this can take many forms: a fan may dress up as their 'hero' – a music star or an actor, for instance – and pretend to be them for a short while. Another fan, however, might dress up as their favourite character in a fantasy film or comic book, and revel in the experience of wearing clothes and make-up that is commonly identified as 'cosplay' – a portmanteau of 'costume' and 'play'. As far as the Hobbiton personalized party is concerned, however, the most fascinating element is not that fans make the effort to dress up in the attire of their favourite characters, and display their loyalty to the narrative and the *LOTR* franchise; this is a common practice among fans, especially those attending fantasy conventions. Indeed, the element worthy of note is that they should do so as part of their celebrations, as part of the ritualized forms of performance that demark their lifestyles and their belonging to a particular group (see Cohen). Any 'celebration', by definition, brings elements of identity with it, both sociologically and culturally.

One may be tempted to suggest that dressing up as a favourite hero or character – 'impersonating' them, as it were – could signal a lack of authenticity in terms of the impersonator's identity, an inability to find a stable sense of individuality that the fan sublimates into taking on the identity of, in the case of *The Lord of the Rings*, the fictional character from Middle-earth. I am aligned with fandom scholar Mark Duffett, however, in suggesting that any form of impersonation – from 'pretending to be' to 'cosplay' – is a practice through which fans 'authenticate themselves' (Duffett 188). Rather than expressing a manifest lack of sociological autonomy, impersonation is more usefully

Figure 5: A wedding marquee in Hobbiton, set up to recall the hobbits' 'party marquee' as shown in the trilogy ©2015, Hobbiton Movie Set Tours.

understood as a 'performative pleasure', a way for the fans to express their sense of individuality through something that they regard to be exciting and important. Simultaneously, the performance affiliates the individual fan with the wider community of the fandom – in this case, the wider scope of *LOTR* fans – therefore validating their choices and their symbolic expressions. In this sense, impersonating the characters of *LOTR* – in an 'authentic' *LOTR* setting such as Hobbiton – is a form of identity-affirmation for the fans.

Immersing oneself in the world of Middle-earth – including wearing clothes that resemble the costumes in the movies, and consuming foods that are reminiscent of those consumed by the characters – is a way of integrating the experience of the Hobbiton set into one's lifestyle: it is, to put it simply, a way of 'owning' Middle-earth, and the adventures and emotions of *The Lord of the Rings* that come with it. For this reason, it is possible to view the experience of the personalized themed party in Hobbtion as a collecting practice, akin to collecting film-related memorabilia that have a particular symbolic and unique value to those who collect them. Unlike merchandise, which is issued 'officially' or 'unofficially' for all to purchase and own, memorabilia have a personal layer to them, and are only important to those who can recognize their significance. Film scholar Kristin Thompson has been keen to point out that fantasy films 'lend themselves to a broad range of merchandising, and fantasy fans tend to collect things' (45). *The Lord of the Rings* franchise, of course, made a virtue of its merchandise potential – placing on sale all sorts of collectible objects, from elven ears to replicas of 'the One Ring' – this intent clearly enhanced by the cinematic genre to which the trilogy belongs.

Memorabilia, on the other hand, belong to the history of the movie itself, its making, its impact, and its diffusion. Memorabilia, as Duffett would put it, are 'intimately linked' to the object of interest (181). Memorabilia, by definition, are something 'of the past', connected to memory and to experience. For this reason, the personalized party in Hobbiton can be included in the circle of movie memorabilia for avid fans. The party in Hobbiton allows fans to become part of the history of the movie set: it opens the narrative of the films to becoming 'theirs', even for just a short period of time. The exclusivity of the experience is made even more memorable by the fact that, in all likelihood, photographs of the event will be taken, constructing a distinct cinematic metanarrative that connects the experience of the set itself – that sense of 'being there' – with the historical uniqueness of memorabilia, and the personalized and intimate nature of the fan practice.

Concluding remarks: An authentic 'party business'?

The differentiation between symbolic and economic capital becomes blurred in the Hobbiton party experience. Truthfully, visiting Hobbiton in itself could be perceived as a reasonably 'lowbrow' experience, as far as fandom is concerned. Anyone can visit Hobbiton, as long as they are willing to pay the price of entry. Even though a considerable effort is still required to actually reach the movie set – not least because it is located in New Zealand, and, for most fans, international travel is most likely required – the experience is open to all, and does not require further engagement than simply being there at the right time. If one wanted to be reminded of Bourdieu's argument on the types of capital in cultural production, one would see symbolic capital as mostly concerned with highbrow experience, whith economic capital being primarily reducible to monetary valuation, and therefore inevitably 'lowbrow'.

The personalized themed parties, however, add a layer of legitimacy to the Hobbiton experience that is not, strictly speaking, made available to the fan masses. Hosting one's own party at Hobbiton requires an engagement that goes beyond the limits of the everyday fan; still, as fan experiences go, it cannot be regarded as a 'highbrow' practice, such a being given access to 'inaccessible' areas, including being backstage when the trilogy was being filmed, or even having a real-life conversation with the director of the movies. In the world of fandom, having a personalized *LOTR*-themed party in Hobbiton could be labelled as a 'middlebrow experience': accessible, but not accessible to all. As far as participatory fandom is concerned, the bespoke party combines 'spectacle with originality, and creative inspiration with cliché' (Shefrin 265). It is, to put it simply, a fandom experience that lies somewhere in between restricted and large scale, its symbolic capital far exceeding that of a simple 'visitor tour' of Hobbiton, and revealing the extent to which intellectual engagement builds the foundation for the fan experience. The financial implications that ensue from the symbolic capital attributed to Hobbiton as a celebration venue clearly add to its importance in economic structures, and uncover a clearer meaning for the expression 'party business'. ●

GO FURTHER

Books

Understanding Fandom: An Introduction to the Study of Media Fan Culture
Mark Duffett
(London: Bloomsbury, 2013)

Symbolic Construction of Community
Anthony P. Cohen
(London: Routledge, 2001)

Practical Reason: On the Theory of Action
Pierre Bourdieu
(Redwood City: Stanford University Press, 1998)

Toward a Critique of the Political Economy of the Sign
Jean Baudrillard
(St. Louis: Telos Press, 1973)

Extracts/Essays/Articles

'One Ring, Many Circles: The Hobbiton Tour Experience and a Spatial Approach to Media Power'
Robert Moses Peaslee
In *Tourist Studies*. 11: 1 (2011), pp. 37–53.

'Constructing the "Cinematic Tourist": the "Sign Indutry" of *The Lord of the Rings*'
Rhodanthi Tzanelli
In *Tourist Studies*. 4:1 (2004), pp. 21–42.

'*Lord of the Rings, Star Wars*, and Participatory Fandom: Mapping New Congruencies between the Internet and Media Entertainment Culture'
Elana Shefrin
In *Critical Studies in Media Communication*. 21: 3 (2004), pp. 261–281

'Fantasy, Franchises, and Frodo Baggins: *The Lord of the Rings* and Modern Hollywood'
Kristin Thompson
In *The Velvet Light Trap*. 52 (2003), pp. 45–63.

On Party Business: True-fan Celebrations in New Zealand's Middle-earth
Lorna Piatti-Farnell

'Indexing, Dragging and the Social Construction of Tourist Sights'
Chris Rojek
In Chris Rojek and John Urry (eds). *Touring Cultures: Transformations of Travel and Theory* (London/New York: Routledge, 1997), pp. 52–74.

Websites

Hobbiton Movie Set Tours: www.hobbitoutours.com

Universal Studios Hollywood: www.universalstudioshollywood.com

Warner Bros. Studio Tour London: The Making of Harry Potter: www.wbstudiotour.co.uk

New Zealand, Home of Middle-earth: www.nzhomeofmiddleearth.com)

Films

The Lord of the Rings: The Return of the King, Peter Jackson (New Zealand/USA: New Line Cinema, 2003).

The Lord of the Rings: The Fellowship of the Ring, Peter Jackson (New Zealand/USA: New Line Cinema, 2001).

'FOOL OF A TOOK!' HE GROWLED. 'THIS IS A SERIOUS JOURNEY, NOT A HOBBIT WALKING-PARTY.'

GANDALF TO PIPPIN IN J.R.R. TOLKIEN'S *THE FELLOWSHIP OF THE RING*

Fan Appreciation
Shaun Gunner, President of the Tolkien Society

Interview by Lorna Piatti-Farnell

Lorna Piatti-Farnell (LPF): *I suppose we should start with the obvious… as the Chairman of the Tolkien Society, and therefore an expert on the* Lord of the Rings *books, what was your reaction to the film trilogy?*

Shaun Gunner (SG): I first saw the films many years before I became the Chairman of the Society – before, in fact, I was even a member. I was just 13 when *The Fellowship of the Ring* [2001] was released and I was instantly captivated. I was entranced. I devoured everything about the films. I bought every film tie-in book. I would visit *TheOneRing.net* three times a day just to find out even the most trivial of film-related gossip. To me, it represented the pinnacle of film production. The very essence of Tolkien had been brought alive.

I take a more pragmatic approach now. I'm more well-read on Tolkien and I feel more attuned to the changes made from the book. Saying that, I still regard *The Fellowship of the Ring* as an excellent film whilst I very much enjoy *The Return of the King* [2003]. I always found *The Two Towers* [2002] a little boring as a rather unexciting 'filler' film in the trilogy. In all three films there are some cracking lines from the characters that I so wish had been said by the characters in the book – 'Stand, Men of the West' by Aragorn is a case in point.

LPF: *In general terms, how do you think the film trilogy was received by the fans of Tolkien's books? What were the most common points of discussion?*

SG: Some groups were very hostile, focusing exclusively on the changes from the book. Others greeted it with unabated enthusiasm, seeing the films as a huge triumph of Tolkien's imagination. There has always been this tension in the Tolkien community – and it's never been fully resolved – but I would say that debates are less heated now than they used to be. What is interesting is how the release of the *Hobbit* films has led to a slight revision of some fans' views of *The Lord of the Rings*: many regard the *Hobbit* films as far worse an adaptation that is too focused on CGI and action scenes to the detriment of Tolkien's story – this has led to a 'softening' of the view on the *Lord of the Rings* trilogy.

I think it is fair to say that visually the vast majority of fans would agree that the films look like Middle-earth: no one argues that Bag End, Gandalf, Isengard or the Dead Men of Dunharrow are inauthentic portrayals. Even if someone imagines Rivendell differently pretty much everyone accepts that its portrayal on-screen was legitimate and well-executed. This was probably helped by having the well-known artists John Howe and Alan

Fan Appreciation
Shaun Gunner, President of the Tolkien Society

Lee as concept designers for the films – their works are highly regarded by Tolkien fans.

Debate amongst Tolkien fans focused very heavily on character changes and, to a lesser extent, plot changes. With regard to characters, what's particularly noted is the heightened 'wimpiness' of Frodo, the level of self-doubt of Aragorn, and Faramir's initial desire for the Ring. Faramir is an incredibly popular character in the story for his noble response to Frodo and Sam: the change in his storyline upset a lot of Tolkien fans.

Some changes from the storyline have actually gone fairly unchallenged: elves at the Battle of Helm's Deep seems to have been an uncontroversial change, for example. And, actually, the removal of Tom Bombadil and the Scouring of the Shire have been widely accepted, compared with, for example, the decision to create the Eye of Sauron (which is widely criticized by Tolkien fans).

LPF: *Are you surprised by the fact that the* LOTR *film trilogy became such a worldwide phenomenon?*

SG: Not at all. *The Lord of the Rings* is one of the best-selling books ever written so it clearly has mass appeal: it's unsurprising that the films would have the same appeal. Tolkien is one of the greatest authors that the United Kingdom has ever produced: he is up there with Shakespeare, Jane Austen and Charles Dickens. His books are already a worldwide phenomenon so it is not at all surprising that the films would be as well.

What does surprise me is that *LOTR* fandom has, to a certain extent, become completely separate from Tolkien fandom more generally. It surprises me that the films have inspired people who not only have no knowledge of the books but who have no interest in gaining that knowledge. There is a general – and, from my perspective, frustrating – lack of imagination as well: so instead of people imagining Legolas they will simply draw Orlando Bloom as Legolas. The omnipresence of imagery can distress some Tolkien fans as much as the films themselves.

LPF: *Inevitably, I feel we need to talk about* The Hobbit... *what are your thoughts on the new film trilogy? And how does it compare to the original (so to speak)* LOTR *trilogy?*

SG: First of all I have no problem with it being a trilogy: *The Hobbit* book was written for children and is in a completely different style from *The Lord of the Rings*. What this does mean is that distances which take 200 pages in *The Lord of the Rings* are covered in just a chapter in *The Hobbit* – so there was definitely space to make the book into multiple films. The films don't feel unnecessarily 'stretched' to me and I think it is disingenuous to claim Jackson has done this for the money – I can't believe he is short of cash!

I thought the first film was fundamentally true to the spirit of the book, albeit I found it a little slow-going. Both films could certainly do with a little editing. I don't object to the amount of CGI as such, but I do think there are a couple of scenes that were a little unnecessary (like the rabbits of Rhosgobel).

Jackson personally had a very difficult task in marrying *The Hobbit* book (very different from all of Tolkien's other writings in Middle-earth) with his own pre-existing *Lord of the Rings* films. At times it feels as if he's done this well – Mirkwood and Goblin-town are good examples of this – at other times I am left wondering whether the *Hobbit* trilogy is actually taking place in the same universe. But I respect Jackson for what he's done – I have a huge amount of respect for him in bringing my favourite books to film. It's easy to sit in an ivory tower and say, 'Those Jackson films are evil because they changed Tolkien' – I don't think that. I think we owe Jackson an enormous debt in the way he has introduced Tolkien to new audiences that Tolkien would never have reached otherwise.

LPF: *How do you feel about the reach of the* LOTR *film trilogy into participatory fandom? I am thinking here of the 'obsession' over visiting the film locations, the film tourism that has made New Zealand a much loved destination… as Middle-earth, of course.*

SG: I think it's great – in fact I would very much like to visit the locations myself! What does disappoint me slightly is the lack of interest in visiting the places that genuinely inspired Tolkien: Sarehole and the Warwickshire countryside, for example. They may not have been as glamorously portrayed on film but they are far more important in creating Tolkien's vision (even the vision vicariously presented on-screen by Jackson). I don't mind the idea that New Zealand is home to the *Lord of the Rings* trilogy, but I do mind the suggestion that it is the 'true' home of Middle-earth. ●

Chapter
06

There, Here and Back Again: The Search for Middle-earth in Birmingham

Emily M. Gray

→ Prologue: I grew up in Walsall, a town on the edge of the Black Country that was famous during the industrial age for its saddles and fancy leather goods. Twenty years ago Birmingham was a city that privileged the car and roads were located above the pavement so that pedestrians had to navigate a warren of subways to get around the city. For this small(ish)-town girl, Birmingham had the big-city buzz, tall buildings and department stores, and sprawling suburbs full of places to go.

I was something of a *flâneur* and would walk around the city for hours listening to music. Led Zeppelin were often my companion and I loved to walk to 'Ramble On' (1969), the rhythm of the song providing the perfect walking pace. Their lyrics seemed so mystical and conjured up ancient times and battles and I wondered from where they drew their inspiration...

Mine's a tale that can't be told, my freedom I hold dear.
How years ago in days of old when magic ruled the air.
T'was in the darkest depths of Mordor, I met a girl so fair,
But Gollum, and the evil one crept up and slipped away with her.
(Page and Plant)

I also loved the song 'Misty Mountain Hop' (1971) from Led Zeppelin's untitled fourth album and my enthusiasm for the band led me to discover Tolkien and *The Lord of the Rings*. It was not until many years later that I discovered Tolkien's Birmingham connection and years after that that I travelled to Aotearoa New Zealand and saw for myself the epic scenery that inspired Peter Jackson's cinematic retelling of Tolkien's best-known work of fiction.

In this chapter I will explore my ongoing fascination with Tolkien's the *Lord of the Rings* trilogy and will link Middle-earth to my English home in the Midlands. I will also explore how *The Lord of the Rings* has contributed to my love of Aotearoa New Zealand, examining throughout how connection to place can shape our imaginations. Finally, in the shadow of Birmingham's 'Tolkien Trail', I will ask why there is a need amongst fans for an 'authentic' Middle-earth experience.

Tolkien and the Birmingham imaginary

Tolkien's connection to Oxford is well known and documented. Less well known is that the author spent much of his childhood in the city of Birmingham, located in the Midlands of England and surrounded by the Shire counties. Far from the minds of many tourists visiting Britain, what was once the centre for British automobile production is now a lively post-industrial city famous as the home of Cadbury's chocolate, heavy metal music, Spaghetti Junction and the Bull Ring shopping mall. Birmingham is proud of its Tolkien connection and the *Birmingham Heritage Forum* claims the author as one of the city's own, stating on the website's homepage that Tolkien is 'one of Birmingham's most important and popular writers'. Such a claim is interesting given that Tolkien left Birmingham for the spires of Oxford in 1911 and never again lived in the city. He returned briefly in 1916 whist on leave from the army during World War I, staying with his wife at the Plough and Harrow Hotel on the Hagley Road, near to the Birmingham Oratory where, as a child, he had been an altar boy. A plaque commemorates this visit even though it predates Tolkien's literary publications by a number of years.

There, Here and Back Again: The Search for Middle-earth in Birmingham
Emily M. Gray

Figure 1: The Plough and Harrow Hotel © 2015, Emily Gray.

Despite its brevity, Tolkien's time in Birmingham was formative and characterized by loss. Following the death of his father in 1895 his mother, Mabel Tolkien, took her two young sons from their home in South Africa to live with relatives in Sarehole, then a hamlet, now part of the Hall Green area of Birmingham. In 1904 Mabel Tolkien died, leaving guardianship of her sons to Father Francis Xavier, Morgan of the Birmingham Oratory. Humphrey Carpenter's 1977 comprehensive biography of Tolkien tells us that following their mother's death, the Tolkien boys left their home in the Moseley area of the city where they had lived with their mother during the latter part of her life, to live in a series of boarding homes closer to the city centre. Loss, or the fear of loss, is a theme of Tolkien's *Lord of the Rings* trilogy and we might think of Gandalf in particular as father figure to the hobbits, a father returned to his children. Given the losses endured by Tolkien as a child it is interesting to note that death is an impermanent state within his Middle-earth creation.

Figure 2: Blue plaque at the Plough and Harrow © 2015, Emily Gray.

Despite their connection to loss, Tolkien's love of the places of his childhood are well documented by biographers such as Humphrey Carpenter, and it is said that as a young man Tolkien enjoyed exploring the area within which he lived. Places like Sarehole Mill, Moseley Bog and the Clent, Lickey and Malvern Hills of Worcestershire, were the inspiration for many of the locations of his fiction, including his aunt's farm, Bag End, the name of which will have a familiar ring to any fan. The hills of Tolkien's youth remain as green and pleasant and roll towards Wales as inexorably as they would have when he experienced them. Birmingham, however, was the fastest growing English city of the nineteenth century and would have changed a lot during Tolkien's childhood, with the middle-class suburbs he inhabited being absorbed into the expanding sprawl. The city's growth was no doubt spurred on by the Industrial Revolution that had begun a century before in the nearby Shropshire town of Ironbridge. The fires of industry quickly spread to the villages and towns nearby, and to the world beyond. During the Industrial Revolution the smog from the many factories and foundries permeated the air and led to the region being unofficially re-named 'The Black Country'. Although Birmingham is not recognized as a part of the Black Country itself, the city was surrounded by it and during the latter part of the nineteenth and early part of the twentieth century large-scale manufacturing arrived into Birmingham, and so Tolkien would have witnessed first-hand the impact of rapid industrial development upon the city.

It is not difficult, therefore, to link my homeland to Tolkien's Middle-earth. Tolkien's lamentation of the effects of industry upon the natural world is a theme of the *Lord of the Rings* trilogy. The encroaching fires of Isengard that wreak havoc upon the gentle countryside are illustrative of the author's feelings about industrialization and its impact not only upon nature but also upon people: Sauron is corrupted partly by the allure of the power that industry brings to him.

The very name Middle-earth is itself evocative of the industrialized Midlands, with

Figure 3: Perrotts Folly ©
2015, Emily Gray.

Figure 4: The Edgbaston
Waterworks Tower © 2015,
Emily Gray.

their belching factories, air thick with the metallic smell of industry and the hissing sounds of pistons travelling on the wind. Because the Industrial Revolution so shaped the world in its current guise, the Midlands were literally at the centre of the industrial world. Birmingham is surrounded by the Black Country, which was, by all accounts, a hellish landscape in its heyday that was 'black by day and red by night'; this famous quote comes from an 1869 volume entitled *Walks in the Black Country* by Elihu Burritt, and captures the effect of industrialization upon place that is reflected within *The Lord of the Rings*. There is further evidence of Birmingham's impact upon Tolkien to be found in the Edgbaston area of the city where Perrotts Folly and the Edgbaston Waterworks Tower sit side-by-side. Located within five minutes walk of each other, these city landmarks are widely understood to be Tolkien's inspiration for the two towers in *The Lord of the Rings*, Saruman's Orthanc and the Eye of Sauron.

Tolkien's dismay at the havoc wreaked upon the natural world by industry then peppers his narrative within *The Lord of the Rings*, whether it is Saruman's destruction of Fangorn Forest or the hobbits' return to Bag End following their adventures. It could also be argued that the juxtaposition in his work between the rural idyll and the industrial destruction of nature reflects the loss of his parents and the move from the rural outskirts of Birmingham to the industrial centre (for more on this see www.tolkienlibrary.com). Such a sorrow connected to place is illustrated in a latter chapter of *The Return of the King* (1955) entitled 'The Scouring of the Shire', where we see Frodo, Sam, Pippin and Merry return to their much changed home,

> Many of the houses that they had known were missing. Some seemed to have been burned down. The pleasant row of old Hobbit holes in the bank to the north side of the Pool were deserted, and their little gardens that used to run down bright to the water's edge were rank with weeds. Worse, there was a whole line of the ugly new houses all along Pool Side [...] an avenue of trees had stood there. They were all gone. And looking with dismay towards Bag End they saw a tall chimney of brick in the distance. It was pouring out black smoke into the evening air. (Tolkien 307)

As alluded to earlier, loss or the fear of loss is an enduring theme of Tolkien's work and of his life – as well as losing both parents by the age of 12 he lost many friends on the battlefields of World War I, the first mechanized war also arguably shaping his narrative within *The Lord of the Rings*. The passage above reflects the irreversible damage done to place by industrialization and war. Tolkien's work however is also full of hope and I would like to think that places, and the people in them, shaped that hope. The following passage from *The Fellowship of the Ring* (1954) illustrates the quiet hopefulness that underpins Tolkien's work: 'The world is indeed full of peril, and in it there are many dark places; but still there is much that is fair; and though in all lands love is now mingled with grief, it grows perhaps the greater' (Tolkien 391).

There, Here and Back Again: The Search for Middle-earth in Birmingham
Emily M. Gray

The *Lord of the Rings* trilogy is, as much as anything, a tale about friendship, and the bonds between people and place. Frodo and the other hobbits set out on their epic journey to save their Shire home, to preserve their way of life. The losses suffered by all of the members of the Fellowship makes them stronger in their bonds to each other and to the lands that they pass through and belong to. The themes of loss, the impact of industrialization upon the natural world and the horror of mechanized war endure within Peter Jackson's cinematic retelling of *The Lord of the Rings*. Jackson imagines the impact of these key themes upon his home of Aotearoa New Zealand, a place relatively unscathed by war and industry. The forests of Paradise and Glenorchy in the South Island are digitally hacked down and a landscape 'black by day and red by night' put in their place. Such imagery is powerful and, for me, links Birmingham to Aotearoa New Zealand.

Interlude
At the age of 32 I left Walsall to live elsewhere for the first time in my life and came to live in Australia. My Australian partner has Maori fish hooks tattooed onto one of her arms, and when we first got together asking her why resulted in an ongoing love affair with Aotearoa New Zealand. Four years and three visits to New Zealand later we are driving around the South Island, me clutching *'The Lord of the Rings' Location Guidebook* (2011) directing my long-suffering lover towards the site of the orc pile in *The Two Towers* (2002), to Isengard, Fangorn Forest, the Misty Mountains, through Rohan and finally to Minas Tirith. The landscape is spectacular; it is beautiful, desolate and haunting all at once. I am enchanted by the Remarkables, a mountain range just outside of the skiing mecca of Queenstown, and delighted to learn that they form the backdrop to Minas Tirith in the movies of *The Lord of the Rings*.

In his foreword to Ian Brodie's *'The Lord of the Rings' Location Guidebook*, Peter Jackson, director of the movie adaptations of the trilogy writes,

Eighteen years old and reading JRR Tolkien for the first time, I was sitting on a train as it left Wellington and rumbled up through the North Island. During the twelve-hour journey, I'd lift my eyes from the book and look at the familiar landscape – which all of a sudden looked like Middle-earth […] there was never any question the film wouldn't be made here. With the variety of landscapes of such an awesome nature […] it was the only way to go. (Jackson, cited in Brodie, iv)

Aotearoa New Zealand has become synonymous with Middle-earth, with Jackson's adaptations of both the *Lord of the Rings* trilogy and *The Hobbit* being filmed there. Tourists flying into Auckland or Wellington will see huge sculptures of dwarves and Gollum and signs declaring Aotearoa New Zealand to be the 'Gateway to Middle-earth'. Birmingham is off the radar as far as the majority of *Lord of the Rings* fandom goes, its scenery scarred by industry and the city's sprawl merging in all directions with the towns of the Black Country. Add to that a 2008 poll by *The Telegraph* voted the Brummie accent as the 'least cool' of the British accents, plus the fact that many fans of *The Lord of the Rings* are so because of the movies, not the books, and we are not left with much in the way of a recipe for tie-in tourism. Birmingham, however, is my city, it colours my memories and influences my speech, it is part of the *Lord of the Rings* mythology, its landmarks as vivid for Tolkien as they are for anyone who has lived in it and loved it. It is important to acknowledge my attachment to Birmingham here, and my nostalgia for a place that I no longer live. For me, the Midlands *are* Middle-earth, the area is bound to Tolkien, to music, scenery and my youth in a way that is unreasonable to expect any fan not from the region to feel or understand. The landscapes of Aotearoa New Zealand provide a familiarity because their celluloid presence is so visceral, and so recognizable in comparison to Sarehole Mill, Mosely Bog or the two towers of Edgbaston.

The road to Middle-earth?

My own love of Tolkien and *The Lord of the Rings* comes partly from my connection to place and my nostalgia for the landscape that shaped my formative years as well as to places that have shaped more recent memories. Fandom is a complex thing in this way – our love of particular cultural outputs are shaped by more than genre or storyline or leading actors, they are shaped by the personal, by memory and nostalgia. That Peter Jackson remembered his fist reading of Tolkien as taking place within the land that he grew up in is significant to why and how he made the movies in the way that he did.

For many of us, to be 'a fan' is about much more than simply liking something because it is good. Our tastes reveal something about who we are, where we come from, how we think. Henry Jenkins convincingly argues in his 2006 book *Fans, Bloggers and Gamers: Exploring Participatory Culture* that contemporary fandom is participatory, and that fan-fiction, online communities, conventions and conferences provide fans with the opportunity to participate in the ongoing construction of their favourite popular culture texts.

There, Here and Back Again: The Search for Middle-earth in Birmingham
Emily M. Gray

Figure 6: Treebeard at the
Custard Factory, Birmingham
© 2015, Emily Gray.

Tie-in tourism has become popular with fans seeking an embodied experience with the sites of their favourite books, movies and TV shows. There is now, for example, *Sex and the City* (1998-2004) tours of New York, *Breaking Bad* (2008-2013) tours of Albuquerque and, Gunhild Agger tells us, tourists in Copenhagen seeking out the seamier locations of *The Killing* (2007-2012), wishing to turn 'sites into sights'. Such a turning of site into sight is illustrative of the power of the visual image and the social theorist Henry Giroux, in his 1994 book *Disturbing Pleasures*, argues that people use visual images as points of recognition, and that popular culture enables people to 'exchange information, listen, feel their desires and expand capacities for joy, love, solidarity and struggle' (210). Being part of a fan community epitomizes Giroux's hopes; in many ways being a fan is about being with others.

Authenticity is also important to fandom; it gives credibility to the story one can tell about a favourite text or set of texts. John Fiske, in a book chapter entitled 'The Cultural Economy of Fandom', published in 1992, argues that authenticity is appropriated by fans as a way to demonstrate their commitment to a particular cultural artefact. The epic scenery of Aotearoa New Zealand provides the *Lord of the Rings* fans with an 'authentic' experience of the cinematic version of Middle-earth. In Birmingham there is a 'Tolkien Trail' that encompasses Sarehole Mill, Mosley Bog and a giant Treebeard sculpture that takes up residence in the former Bird's Custard Factory, now a centre for arts and digital media.

The sites/sights on the 'Tolkien Trail' require the use of imagination – because of Birmingham's industrial past and post industrial present, many of the places bear little resemblance to Tolkien's experience of them and, compared to the unspoilt drama of the landscapes of Aotearoa New Zealand, they require more work on behalf of the fan.

The proud Midlander in me wants to reclaim Middle-earth, to argue that its roots are in and around Birmingham and that this is where authenticity is. However Middle-earth was pieced together by Tolkien from fragments of memory and experience and, most of all, from the imagination. *The Lord of the Rings* is a work of fantasy and as such has no definitive core, no authentic home except that which lives over the hills and far away within the imagination, J. R. R. Tolkien's, Peter Jackson's and our own. ●

~~~~~~~~~~~~

GO FURTHER

Books

'The Lord of the Rings' Location Guidebook
Ian Brodie
(Auckland: Harper-Collins, 2011)

Fans, Bloggers and Gamers: Exploring Participatory Culture
Henry Jenkins
(New York/London: New York University Press, 2006)

Disturbing Pleasures: Learning Popular Culture
Henry A. Giroux
(London: Routledge, 1994)

'The Lord of the Rings': 50ᵗʰ Anniversary One-Volume Collection
J. R. R. Tolkien
(Boston/New York: Houghton Mifflin Harcourt, 1994 [1954–55])

J. R. R. Tolkien: A Biography
Humphrey Carpenter
(Boston/New York: Houghton Mifflin Harcourt, 1987 [1977])

Extracts/Essays/Articles

'The Killing': Urban Topographies of a Crime
Gunhild Agger
In *Journal of Popular Television*. 1: 2 (2013).

'The Cultural Economy of Fandom'
John Fiske
In Lisa A. Lewis (ed.). *The Adoring Audience: Fan Culture and Popular Media* (London: Routledge, 1992).

Online

'Brummie Accent Voted Least Cool in Britain'
Chris Irvine

There, Here and Back Again: The Search for Middle-earth in Birmingham
Emily M. Gray

The Telegraph. 24 September 2008, www.telegraph.co.uk/news/topics/howabout-that/307382/Brummie-accent-voted-least-cool-in-Britain.html,

Websites

Tolkien Library: www.tolkienlibrary.com

Songs

'Misty Mountain Hop'
Jimmy Page, Robert Plan and Jon Paul Jones
(Atlantic Records, 1971)

'Ramble On'
Jimmy Page and Robert Plant
(Atlantic Records, 1969)

'THERE IS ONLY ONE LORD OF THE RING, ONLY ONE WHO CAN BEND IT TO HIS WILL. AND HE DOES NOT SHARE POWER.'

GANDALF IN PETER JACKSON'S *THE FELLOWSHIP OF THE RING*

Chapter
07

Looking for Lothíriel: The Presence of Women in Tolkien Fandom

Cait Coker and Karen Viars

→ Many people assume that the *Lord of the Rings* fandom began with the Peter Jackson film adaptations rather than with Tolkien's books themselves; further, they often assume (and not without a great deal of evidence) that the majority of fans creating fanworks are teen girls writing Mary Sue romances with Legolas Greenleaf. Despite its paucity of heroines, *LOTR* fandom online seemed to consist overwhelmingly of women writing about male characters' relationships either with each other or with original female characters.

Before we proceed further, we must remember two keys to understanding *LOTR* fandom over time: that it *does* take place over time, in that the novels have a 60-year history and that people – particularly women – have been writing about and interacting with the texts from the start, and that the film fandom may have adopted a specific canon of events, but the practices and preoccupations of the fans are largely the same.

An axiom of fan studies is that fanworks are interpretive and analytical acts that reveal insights into an original text through its reception by the audience. The larger body of critical work on fans has focused on contemporary fandom – fans in the age of the Internet with the ability to quickly and inexpensively share works of art and fiction. This attitude ignores the long history of Tolkien's texts and in some ways its biggest Big Name Fans – namely Peter Jackson, Fran Walsh and Philippa Boyens, the co-creators of the *LOTR* films. Though a great deal has been written about the movies, the presence, or rather, the absence, of Jackson's women partners in discussions is noticeable, casting an emphasis on male creation that is not necessarily present. If we are to view the *Lord of the Rings* films as fan adaptations – which themselves have fan adaptations – we have to read them in the same way that we read the other 'unofficial texts': as in dialogue with Tolkien himself and as in dialogue with the culture of their creation.

Women in *LOTR* book fandom

If we go back further in time, we can see a similar pattern of women writing about *LOTR* in print-zines; they, too, seemed to outnumber the male fans, and chose to write fiction and essays that brought women to the fore of the stories. The earliest Tolkien fanworks appeared in the late 1950s, only a few years after the *LOTR* novels appeared in both the United Kingdom and the United States. They are documented at length by Sumner Gary Hunnewell, who has tirelessly worked to identify individual citations and fanzines detailing early Tolkien fandom from 1959 through 1968, with yet more bibliographies undoubtedly forthcoming. These first fanworks share many concerns with contemporary fandom, including speculation about Tolkien's worlds – it is worth noting that fan versions of *The Silmarillion* (J. R. R. Tolkien, 1977) appeared well before the promised books – and the private lives of his characters. Like most mid-century fan activities, publication fanzine runs were small and often identi-

Figure 1: 'Princess Lothíriel'
© 2014, Francesco Amadio.

Looking for Lothíriel: The Presence of Women in Tolkien Fandom
Cait Coker and Karen Viars

fied with specific individuals. Perhaps the most well-known Tolkien fan of the day was science fiction author Marion Zimmer Bradley, who published several Tolkien-related works, including the fanzine *Anduríl*; the short story 'A Meeting in the Hyades' in which her own hero Regis Hastur, the protagonist of her novel *The Sword of Aldones* (1962), meets Aragorn; the essay 'Men, Halflings, and Hero Worship', which analyses both the character and characterization of Éowyn; and the novelette *The Jewel of Arwen*, which originally appeared in her fanzine and later as a small chapbook.

While Bradley was a professional author in her own right, many (most) fans are not; further, the vast majority of fan writings are not and will not be read by others outside of the close-knit circles of fan writers. All the same, many Tolkien fans pride themselves on the technical skill level of their work, researching and extrapolating from the canon to create fanworks that can be read as seamlessly as possible against the original tales. Tolkien had a polite relationship with his fans, though he was never quite comfortable with how the books were adopted by the counter-culture movement. He wrote in a Letter of Comment to the fanzine *Triode*, 'I am myself a member of the amorphous body of "fandom": but I am afraid I do not often come across anything nowadays that seems very readable' (Tolkien 27). The question of 'readability' and fan texts is a longstanding debate, especially since Tolkien's estate has had a far less lackadaisical relationship with fandom than Tolkien himself. For example, when Bradley republished *The Jewel of Arwen* in her 1985 collection, *The Best of Marion Zimmer Bradley*, the Tolkien estate claimed infringement and the story was removed from all subsequent printings.

While some tensions arise from copyright and legal issues, other tensions in Tolkien fandom often focus on the textual 'purity' of the work, often emphasizing a hierarchy of quality and adherence to Tolkien's legendarium. Thus there is a rather divisive split between the book fandom and the film fandom, often centering on the presence of women. For many years, it was an unspoken requisite that the 'quality' of works was based heavily on book characters and knowledge; as such, canonical women characters such as Arwen, Éowyn, Rosie Cotton and Lothíriel were 'permissible' because they were Tolkien's characters. Lothíriel was especially interesting as she was literally a footnote in the Appendices; readers knew only that she was Èomer's wife, that she was the daughter of Prince Imrahil, and that her son was named Elfwine. Fan writers were therefore free to ascribe to her whatever characteristics they desired for the purpose of their stories: she could be a quiet and knowledgeable healer, a feisty would-be shield maiden, a willing or a reluctant bride. With the advent of film fandom in 2001, attitudes towards women characters and how they were presented would shift again through the new exposure of Tolkien's work because of the Jackson film adaptations.

Women in the *LOTR* movie fandom
Peter Jackson's film adaptations of *The Lord of the Rings* function similarly to other works of fanfiction: recreating the text as much as possible but adding a new spin. If

Tolkien's novels recast as the major concerns of the mid-twentieth century – industrial growth and world war – then Jackson's films were an echo of those of the early twenty-first century: of terrorism and environmental collapse. But where did this leave the women?

Stephen Colbert introduced the 2014 San Diego ComicCon panel of Peter Jackson and the cast of *The Hobbit: The Desolation of Smaug* (2013) by remembering the earliest news of the *LOTR* films:

> A rumor came to us that director Peter Jackson would be making an adaptation of the trilogy. At the time, many of us knew him only from his movie *Heavenly Creatures*, and as great as that movie is, I wasn't sure there was room for hysterical, murderous teenage girls in Middle-earth [...] other than, of course, Éowyn. [...] And then the movies broke upon the world, and to steal a line from C.S. Lewis, 'Here were beauties that pierced like swords and burned like cold iron.' Here were movies that would break your heart, good beyond hope. And rather than take away our treasure, Peter and Fran Walsh and Philippa Boyens and Richard Taylor and Grant Major and Dan Hennah and the cast and the crew and WETA Digital and the land and the people of New Zealand itself added to our stories, complemented our imagination. (Buchanan)

What Colbert iterates with a light touch we reiterate with a serious one: the *LOTR* films 'added' and 'complemented' the legendarium. The *LOTR* films have indubitably achieved popculture recognition, and they have changed the landscape of fandom in doing so.

Jackson's adaptations made some critical alterations in female characters' roles, which many longtime book fans found problematic: Galadriel as narrator, Rosie Cotton as barmaid, Arwen as Frodo's rescuer rather than Glorfindel, to name just a few. Female characters had more agency, and their actions contributed more directly to the journey to destroy the Ring. Fans who judged the movies based on their fidelity to the source texts found these adjustments objectionable – and sometimes unforgivable. As one fan on an *LOTR* message board noted, 'Thank god PJ [Peter Jackson] didn't put [Arwen] at Helm's Deep. It was bad enough that he felt she needed more involvement than she had in the book' (Shadowman 82).

Fans who became familiar with *LOTR* through the films often have a different perspective than those who know the material through the books. For them, fidelity to Tolkien's vision is *not* the benchmark of quality. Science fiction and fantasy media fans expect adaptations of classic works to offer the same romance, action and intrigue that appear in modern film-making: Christopher Tolkien himself recently gave an interview where he stated,

Looking for Lothíriel: The Presence of Women in Tolkien Fandom
Cait Coker and Karen Viars

They gutted the book, making an action movie for 15–25 year olds. [...] The gap widened between the beauty, the seriousness of the work, and what it has become is beyond me. This level of marketing reduces to nothing the aesthetic and philosophical significance of this work. (Vogt)

Many also expect media adaptations to provide heroines comparable to those they already know and love: women with agency and their own stories, regardless of their portrayal in the source texts. While many book fans decried the changes leading to larger roles for female characters as disloyalty to the text, movie fans were unaware of the changes, at least initially; for them, the female characters' actions were a natural part of the stories. Consequently, fanworks arising from *LOTR* movie fandom embrace female characters' expanded roles and opportunities, decrying the sexism of the book fans, and, supposedly, of Tolkien himself. However, as Anwyn writes,

Figure 2: 'Lothíriel of Dol Amroth' ©2014, neverland300690.

> the text of *Lord of the Rings* does not for a moment bear out the idea that Tolkien had any kind of derogatory opinion about women. Three things are clear: he was far from a misogynist, the female characters in his masterpiece *collectively* represent everything that is great about being a woman, and less representation does not equal less importance (Challis 115).

Éowyn is perhaps the best illustration of such a reading: she defeats the Witch-King of Angmar in combat and is vocal about her resistance to 'traditional' roles of medieval womanhood. (Though Rohirric shield-maidens of the past are referenced, none but Éowyn are seen, either in book or on film.) The *LOTR* films emphasized her heroism, even blatantly configuring her as one of the films' main heroes in the promotional posters for *The Two Towers* (2002).

Treatment of the book–film divide can thus vary greatly. *Archive of Our Own*, one of the largest fanfiction archives online, has separate categories for *LOTR* book and movie fanworks, and others follow suit. Indeed, one fan cautions writers to label movieverse fanfiction clearly to avoid a 'tongue lashing' from book fans, who 'are characteristically a little intolerant of people who haven't read the books'; the purpose of this classification is to allow book fans to avoid movieverse fanfiction. She goes on to advise fan writers not to combine book and movie elements in fanworks because 'they often clash badly' (Dreamingfifi). As we can see here, book fans do not necessarily consider movie adaptations a separate canon, but they do acknowledge the differences that come with those interpretations of character and story. Therefore, the aforementioned questions of textual 'purity' and 'quality' in *LOTR* fandom return to how people read the books versus the movies.

loveless-doll.deviantart.com

Figure 3: 'Princess Lothíriel'
© 2014, Suzana Uhr.

Lothíriel: Healer, warrior, wife

A case study of sorts can be made through the character of Lothíriel. Lothíriel appears in Tolkien's novels as quite literally a footnote in *The Return of the King*: in Appendix A, Part II, 'The House of Eorl', Tolkien writes, 'In the last year of the Third Age he [Èomer] wedded Lothíriel, daughter of Imrahil. Their son Elfwine the Fair ruled after him' (387). In book fandom, Èomer was a fairly minor character, seldom explicated in fanworks or criticism in the same way that Aragorn or Frodo – or indeed, his sister Éowyn – was. On film, however, he was portrayed by Karl Urban, an actor with a devoted following. While his film portrayal was brief, with small points of narrative departure from the texts, fans began to revisit his role in art and fiction – and to speculate about the character who would become his wife.

Given the sparsity of information, Lothíriel could become, to all intents and purposes, an author's original character. She could be like Éowyn, craving freedom and adventure; like Arwen, beautiful and mystical; or like Rosie Cotton, an ideal wife and helpmeet. Because of her origins in the text, she (and her authors) could avoid the often misogynistic accusation of being a 'Mary Sue', a clear and idealized stand-in for the fan author. In contrast, Amy H. Sturgis has written about fandom's various versions of Rosie Cotton, who exists variously as a healer to Samwise Gamgee's wounded spirit and as an antagonist to his romance with Frodo; in short, the fairly typical demonization of women characters who present a block to slash pairings. Èomer, as a minor character, has a smaller slash following than other characters, and as such, romances with him tend towards the heteronormative canon – with his wife. As a romantic lead in various fanfictions, Lothíriel often takes on the appearance and personality of the quintessential romance heroine: slender and lovely, feisty and quick-witted. Sometimes she balks at the prospect of getting married for political alliance only to fall in love with her betrothed, while at other times she and Èomer wed for love from the start.

As studies such as Janice Radway's *Reading the Romance* (1991) and Anne Jamison's *Fic: Why Fanfiction Is Taking Over the World* (2013) have demonstrated, these works reveal the cultural preoccupations of their authors. While the treatment and agency of women were not the top priorities of either Tolkien or Jackson, they are for numerous fan writers. Those who write about Lothíriel navigate the concerns of contemporary women, which include not just the management of romantic relationships and children, but the costs of maintaining independence in a world that all too frequently insists on the erasure of the said independence. Lothíriel is not a Bridget Jones for the *LOTR* set, but she is an obligingly blank space for authors to inscribe their own struggles.

Looking for Lothíriel: The Presence of Women in Tolkien Fandom
Cait Coker and Karen Viars

Conclusion: The road goes ever on

As Jackson's creative team, including Philippa Boyens and Fran Walsh, Jackson's life partner, moved from the *LOTR* trilogy to their next project, *The Hobbit*, they considered the role of women again. Tolkien's earlier novel had no women in it at *all*, which provided a conundrum to the film-makers.

To work toward a solution they added a *Lord of the Rings* character – the ethereal elf Galadriel, played by Cate Blanchett – to the 'hobbit' story. The move prompted a dust-up among some Tolkien fans, but Ms Walsh and Ms Boyens said it was important to them, both as storytellers and as women, to add a female character who could bring more emotional depth to the spectacle (Barnes).

And of course, in the second film, they added an original character of their own: the elf Tauriel, played by Evangeline Lilly. Tauriel's appearance in film canon has appalled many book (and film) fans to their cores – but pleased many others. While Tauriel is no Lothíriel, she's no Arwen or Éowyn either. She is, like other fan creations, a voice for the authors. Speaking to Legolas of the growing evil abroad and of the elves' duty to fight it, she asks, 'Are we not part of this world?' This is a question that women characters – and writers and fans – must continually ask of Tolkien and his works. ●

~~~~~~~~~~~~

GO FURTHER

Books

Fic: Why Fanfiction Is Taking Over the World.
Anne Jamison.
(Dallas: Smart Pop Books, 2013)

The Lord of the Rings: The Return of the King
J.R.R. Tolkien
(London: Mariner Books, [1955] 2012)

Reading the Romance: Women, Patriarchy, and Popular Literature
Janice Radway
(Chapel Hill: University of North Carolina Press, 1991)

The Best of Marion Zimmer Bradley
Marion Zimmer Bradley (Martin H. Greenberg, ed.)
(New York: DAW Books, 1985)

Tolkien and the Critics: Essays on J.R.R. Tolkien's The Lord of the Rings
Neil D. Isaacs and Rose A. Zimbardo (eds)
(Baltimore: T-K Graphics, 1973)

The Sword of Aldones
Marion Zimmer Bradley
(New York: Ace Books, 1962)

The Jewel of Arwen
Marion Zimmer Bradley
First published in *I Palantir* 2 (August 1961), pp. 4–17. Reprinted as a chapbook (Baltimore: T-K Graphics, 1974).

Articles/Essays/Extracts

'Middle Earth Wizard's Not-So-Silent Partner'
Brooks Barnes
The New York Times. 2 December 2012, p. AR1.

'Reimagining Rose: Portrayals of Tolkien's Rosie Cotton in Twenty-First Century Fan Fiction'
Amy H. Sturgis.
Mythlore. 93/94 (2006), pp. 166–88.

'Men are from Gondor, Women are from Lothlorien.'
Anwyn
In Erica Challis (ed.). *The People's Guide to J.R.R. Tolkien* (Cold Spring Harbor: Cold Spring Press, 2003), pp. 115–20.

'A Meeting in the Hyades'
Marion Zimmer Bradley
First published in *Andúril* 1 (Summer 1962), pp. 14–29. Reprinted in *Starstone* 1 (January 1978), pp. 26–39.

'Men, Halflings, and Hero Worship'
Marion Zimmer Bradley
First published in *Astra's Tower* 5 (May 1961), p. 2. Reprinted in *Niekas* 16 (June 1966), pp. 25–44.

Looking for Lothíriel: The Presence of Women in Tolkien Fandom
Cait Coker and Karen Viars

'Letter of Comment in *Fan Dance*'
J. R. R. Tolkien
In *Triode*. 18 (May 1960), pp. 354–355.

Online

'Stephen Colbert's Epic Speech About *The Hobbit* Will Thrill Any Tolkien Fan'
Kyle Buchanan
The Vulture. 28 July 2014.
http://www.vulture.com/2014/07/stephen-colbert-hobbit-comic-con-speech.html

'Christopher Tolkien gives rare interview to French newspaper, *Le Monde*'
Josh Vogt
The Examiner. 12 July 2012.
http://www.examiner.com/article/christopher-tolkien-gives-rare-interview-to-french-newspaper-le-monde

Websites

'Arwen at Helm's Deep' Comment
Shadowman 82
The One Ring: The Home of Tolkien Online. 5 July 2014, http://forums.theonering.com/viewtopic.php?f=13&t=106451&p=4077638.

Tolkien Fandom Review: From Its Beginnings to 1964 [Online fanzine]
Sumner Gary Hunnewell
Efanzines.com. 2010, http://efanzines.com/TFR/TolkienFandom2ndEd.pdf.
[More yearly bibliographies are also available, through 1968.]

'From Book to Movie'
Dreamingfifi
Merin Essi ar Quenteli! 2003, http://www.realelvish.net/movies

Films

The Hobbit: The Desolation of Smaug, Peter Jackson, dir. (New Line Cinema, United States/New Zealand: 2013).

'I WOULD RATHER SHARE A LIFETIME WITH YOU, THAN FACE ALL THE AGES OF THIS WORLD ALONE.'

ARWEN IN PETER JACKSON'S *THE FELLOWSHIP OF THE RING*

Chapter
08

Lords of the Franchise: *The Lord of the Rings,* IP Rightsand Policing Appropriation

Paul Mountfort

→ *The Lord of the Rings* occupies the acme of global transmedia franchises, along with such worthies as *Star Wars* (1977-2005) and *Harry Potter* (2001-2011). The books already comprised the second best-selling literary work of all time, with estimated sales of over 150 million copies. Yet the ensuing profits, however large, are like a low-rising foothill when set against the peaks of New Line Cinema's takings, with *The Return of the King* (2003) placed as the seventh highest grossing movie of all time at $US1.1 billion and *The Two Towers* (2002) 28th at $US926 million.

However, as we shall see, if Tolkien had not sold the multimedia rights to Hollywood the films might never have been made. Consequently it is the California-based Saul Zaentz subsidiary Middle-earth Enterprises that wields worldwide control over film, stage, gaming and merchandizing rights. Inevitably, with hundreds of millions of dollars at stake, the tussle over ownership of 'the Ring' has been rancorous, with the heirs to the book rights, Tolkien Estate, and Middle-earth Enterprises aggressively policing their IP (Intellectual Property).

'There is only one lord of the rings […] and he does not share power,' intones Gandalf in *The Fellowship of the Ring* (2001), and the backstory of this franchise is in some ways as gripping as Tolkien's ring saga itself, which in large part reiterates the Old Norse tale of the cursed ring of Andvari, centrepiece of the Nibelungen-hoard, over which brothers slew brothers and dynastic houses fell. The ring functions as an apt metaphor for the IP rights to the lucrative *LOTR* books, films, games and associated media, over which those whom I term the 'lords of the franchise' have battled it out for decades. Moreover, the resulting spectacle can be viewed as a case study illustrating a historic divergence that has opened up in how we frame and engage with popular texts: whereas on the one hand critical theory and pop cultural practice have increasingly converged to regard such mega-narratives as a kind of common property to be appropriated through practices such as fanfiction, cosplay and other forms of homage and parody, the legal position of their IP owners has increasingly hardened. While the big players, such as Tolkien Estate, Middle-earth Enterprises, Saul Zaentz, New Line Cinema and Peter Jackson have been involved in titanic and well-publicized legal stoushes, even minor infringements can see small-time players ending up in lengthy and costly court battles, as copyright holders seek to police unsanctioned appropriations.

This chapter is divided into three parts: the first recalls the events by which, before his death, Tolkien sold the film rights to United Artists in 1969, thereby setting the scene for a fundamental schism in the way in which rights to different media arms of the franchise would be owned, developed and policed. The second surveys some of the downstream effects of this, and in particular the epic battles centring on the production of the Jackson/New Line *LOTR* trilogy of films, and the subsequent fallings-out among parties. While these sections are primarily based on media reports and court filings (there has been little published analysis of the issue to date), the third and concluding section uses my own experience to illustrate how an author of a work drawing on the *LOTR* mythology for a general audience can get caught in the crossfire of this wider IP battlefield.

Sale of the century

The *Lord of the Rings* novels enjoyed a rapid spike in popularity following full publication by Allen and Unwin in 1955. It was not long before the twin spectres of adaptation and the profit-making machinery of modern media franchises began to bear down on the books. In *The Letters of JRR Tolkien* (2012), Tolkien mentions talk of animated film

Lords of the Franchise: *The Lord of the Rings,* IP Rights and Policing Appropriation
Paul Mountfort

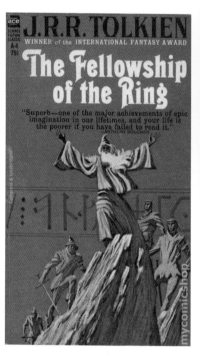

offers as early as 1957, and piracy had become an issue by 1965 with Ace Books's infamous unauthorized US edition.

He wrote to W. H. Auden on 12 May that year of his intention to 'produce a revision of both *The Hobbit* and *The Lord of the Rings* that can be copyrighted and, it is hoped, defeat the pirates'. By 1969, with thoughts of future inheritance taxes partly in mind, the temptation to cut a deal with Hollywood had become too great: Tolkien agreed to sell the film rights for both to United Artists for £100,000 (equivalent to about £2.5 million today) and a 7.5 per cent share of future profits. The Saul Zaentz Company acquired the rights from United Artists, and in turn formed Tolkien Enterprises – now named Middle-earth Enterprises – which to this day licenses the rights not only to film but all non-print media and merchandizing, including board games, computer games and themed goods.

In retrospect the sale was to drive a cleft through the heart of Tolkien's legacy: the two towers, as it were, of the Tolkien Estate and Middle-earth Enterprises slug it out to this day over the destiny of the Ring. For underlying the titanic legal battles are fundamental ideological differences. Tolkien Estate and the associated Tolkien Company retain the book rights to *The Hobbit* and *LOTR,* and still wield full rights to the other content from the Tolkien universe, including such works as *The Silmarillion* (1977) and *The Book of Lost Tales* (1983-1984). As a legal entity, it is comprised of Tolkien's surviving children (Christopher, sole surviving son, executor of his father's will and general director of the Estate, and his sister Pricilla), six grandchildren and eleven great-grandchildren. Regarding themselves as the rightful heirs, the Estate wields ongoing control of print publication through the Tolkien Department located at HarperCollins's head branch in London. It functions in a radically different way from purely commercial IP holders, whose goal is maximum profit. As expressed by grandson Adam Tolkien, 'Normally, the executors of the estate want to promote a work as much as they can [...] But we are just the opposite. We want to put the spotlight on that which is not *Lord of the Rings.*' The Estate and associated Tolkien Company thus act as high priests of the canon, unapologetically purging material that violates the purity of the source texts. As Christopher Tolkien stated in an interview, 'I could write a book on the idiotic requests I have received.' The French daily *Le Monde* (the Estate is physically based in the south of France) concluded, 'He is trying to protect the literary work from the three-ring circus that has developed around it. In general, the Tolkien Estate refuses almost all requests' (12 July 2012).

It is a world away from affairs on the other side of the Atlantic, or rather, the Pacific Coast, where Middle-earth Enterprises is based, in Berkeley, California. Set up by Saul Zaentz following his acquisition of adaptation rights in 1976, it controls the film, stage, gaming and other media and merchandizing rights. The half-forgotten 1978 animated *LOTR* film, directed by Ralph Bakshi, for instance, was funded and produced under

Figure 1: Original US cover of The Fellowship of the Ring.

Figure 2: LEGO toy set for The
Lord of the Rings and Figure
3: Fan illustration of Gollum
with the Ring.

Figure 3: Fan illustration of
Gollum with the Ring.

Saul Zaentz and distributed by United Artists, and a 1982
worldwide licensing deal with Iron Crown Enterprises was
the biggest in the history of role-playing games at the
time. In 1994 New Line Cinema (technically New Line
Film Productions Inc.) was acquired by Turner Broadcast-
ing System, merging with Time Warner in 1996, paving the
way for the Peter Jackson-directed trilogy of 2001–03.
Not only the films and DVDs but all forms of merchandizing rights, especially games and themed goods, have of
course since exploded into multi-billion dollar industries.
The current estimated profits of film and DVD sales are
evenly matched by the merchandise, at about US$3 billion
a piece for a total of $6 billion – equivalent to the annual
GDP of Iceland.

The two towers

The Estate had never been happy with the prospect of a
somewhat freewheeling adaptation by Peter Jackson
defining popular reception of Tolkien's celebrated masterpiece for a generation or more, but it was the runaway
success of the films that paved the road to court for the
two parties. Although sales of the books increased by 1,000 per cent due to the success
of the film trilogy, the billions of dollars in ticket sales and associated profits led the
Estate to revisit the contractual clause that entitled it to 7.5 per cent of profits from any
adaptations. The result was a legal case commencing in 2006 titled 'Christopher Reuel
Tolkien v New Line Cinema Corp'. In response, New Line Cinema's lawyers claimed that
the films did not, in fact, turn a profit (studios often offset production costs of movies against the wider expenses of the studio, leading to some fairly creative account-
ing practices). According to *Bloomberg*, in early 2009 the Tolkien Estate, the Tolkien
Trust and HarperCollins demanded the sum of US$220 million and 'observer rights'
over subsequent adaptations. Settlement was reached in late 2009, and while the ex-
act sums and payments schedule have not been publically disclosed, the Tolkien Estate
was awarded its cut, though crucially not control of subsequent adaptations or merchandise, meaning the 2012–14 New Line/MGM adaptation of *The Hobbit* was free to
go ahead.

Indeed, the first decade and a half of the twenty-first century has seen almost con-
tinual litigation, not only between the Estate and Enterprises, but among the various
parties with a stake in the film and associated profits. Peter Jackson himself sued New
Line in 2005 over the 'miscalculation' of his directorial royalties from *The Fellowship
of the Ring*, also settled for an undisclosed sum. The same year Saul Zaentz weighed in

Lords of the Franchise: *The Lord of the Rings*, IP Rights and Policing Appropriation
Paul Mountfort

Figure 4: A LOTR-inspired creation on Minecraft.

against New Line over his share of the profits, with *Variety* reporting the settlement at USD$186 million. The Estate has also been involved in various downstream legal actions, including, for example, a subpoena in 2007 against eSnips' infringement of its digital rights. Litigation between the Estate and Enterprises continues. As Douglas C. Kane reported on *TheOneRing.net*, in 2012 the former went back to Court with the charge of copyright infringement, with the following filing:

> There are two main activities that plaintiffs claim defendants infringe upon rights that plaintiff assert they still hold: (1) Lord of the Rings themed slot machines; and (2) online and downloadable video games. The basis of the claims is that the original agreement in which the film rights were sold only granted limited merchandising rights that cover 'personal property that can physically be purchased,' and that these activities exceed the scope of those limited merchandising rights. The plaintiffs also claim that Zaentz has been infringing trademark rights.

As we have seen, Middle-earth Enterprises and co. have seldom been slow to resort to litigation themselves; in response to the above, as *TheOneRing.net* further reported, Saul Zaentz and Warner Brothers countersued the Estate, alleging that

> the 'repudiation' of agreement with Estate has prevented [us] from entering into license agreements for online games and casino slot machines in connection with The Hobbit – a form of customary exploitation [we] previously had utilized in connection with the Lord of the Rings trilogy – which has harmed Warner both in the form of lost license revenue and also in decreased exposure for the Hobbit films.

As of the time of writing, this latest battle between the lords of the franchise is ongoing, with potentially hundreds of millions of dollars at stake.

A case study in policing appropriation: *The Lord of the Rings Runes*

The area of fan appropriation per se is too large a subject for this chapter to address, from fanfiction to *Minecraft* (Markus Persson, 2009-present) worlds, but readers should note that, broadly, the Tolkien Estate discourages such appropriations. As they state in their FAQs on www.tolkienestate.com, with regards to whether fans can 'write/complete/develop' their own versions of Tolkien's *Unfinished Tales* (1980):

> The simple answer is NO.
> You are of course free to do whatever you like for your own private enjoyment, but there is no question of any commercial exploitation of this form of 'fan-fiction'.
> [W]e must make it as clear as possible that the Tolkien Estate never has, and never will authorize the commercialisation or distribution of any works of this type.
> The Estate exists to defend the integrity of J.R.R. Tolkien's writings.

While fanfiction writers may wish to avoid antagonizing the Estate through posting 'inappropriate' material (for example, parodies in the homoerotic slash genre), it is *commercial exploitation* that is the real rub, as my own tale of tangling with the lords of the franchise over an unauthorized manuscript illustrates. I offer this as a brief case study of how things can play out for an author who gets caught in the middle of the IP battle between the Estate and Middle-earth Enterprises.

In 2000, while the *LOTR* trilogy directed by Peter Jackson was still being filmed in New Zealand for its 2001 inaugural release, I was a Ph.D. student, working on a thesis titled 'Oracle-texts: the western tradition'. The dissertation looked at systems of popular divination – such as Runes, Ogam and Tarot – as simultaneously archaic and postmodern forms of storytelling media. I had fairly thoroughly researched the use of runes in divination, concluding that while the historical evidence for such use was patchy, contemporary users requisitioned the symbol-set in a kind of appropriation of the cultural mythology connected to the Runes, projecting themselves into the character set and mythological canvass of the Norse gods, mythical beings, powers and forces. The result is a kind of transmediated play. By way of parallel, as Michael Strickmann comments in his landmark study *Chinese Poetry and Prophecy: The Written Oracle in East Asia* (2005):

> Some oracle sequences are shot through with allusions to characters and situations in historical tales, novels and plays. They tacitly invite the person in quest of divine guidance to place himself or herself in the role of the historical or legendary exemplar and act accordingly. The solution to all one's problems is found in a well-known precedent. Even as such-a-one long ago got out of *his* scrape, so now may *you*. (xxi)

In many ways this kind of deep engagement and appropriation is reminiscent of other

Lords of the Franchise: *The Lord of the Rings*, IP Rights and Policing Appropriation
Paul Mountfort

forms of fan practice and participation, including fanfiction, the adoption of gaming avatars and cosplay.

Part of my research was a more specific investigation of the oracle 'guidebook' genre which paradoxically – as I have argued in relation to the Tarot in 'Tarot Guide Books as a Literary Genre' in Emily Auger's *Tarot in Culture* (2014) – may be formulaic in terms of structure but by design facilitate virtually infinite user-generated 'narratives of destiny'. In other words, such texts are implicated in a kind of speculative, future-focused storytelling. In early 2000 I penned a short (30,000 words) guide of this kind that took the Moon Runes of Erebor from *The Hobbit* – essentially an expanded form of the Elder Futhark runescript used in popular rune divination – and assigned to each rune a corresponding character, object, event or scene from *The Lord of the Rings*. For example, in the traditional Elder Futhark script the fourth rune is named Ansuz, which literally means 'a god', and the two medieval Scandinavian rune-poems suggest that it refers to Odin ('the king of Valhalla'). This cloaked, staff-wielding god is widely recognized as one of the inspirations for Tolkien's Gandalf. So when adapting the 'meanings' of the Moon Runes from the traditional Elder Furthark Runes I substituted Gandalf for Odin, and replaced the Old Norse references with verses composed by Frodo in reminiscence of Gandalf from *The Fellowship of the Ring*:

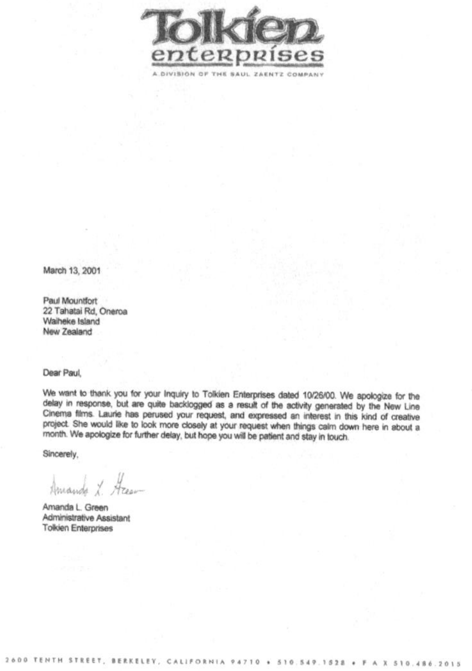

A Lord of wisdom throned he sat
Swift in anger, quick to laugh
An old man with a battered hat
who leaned upon a thorny staff (404).

Similarly the rune identified with a 'river-fish' in the *Anglo-Saxon Rune-Poem*, which is described as living in water but taking its food on land, seemed like a logical choice for Gollum, whose mythological roots lie in a strange kind of liminal creature, related to the quasi-mythological figure of the otter in Norse myth's *Volsunga Saga*. The work was aimed at youthful fans of *LOTR*, as a way of personalizing engagement with Tolkien's mythological universe.

In any case, when completed I sent the manuscript – tentatively titled *The Lord of the Rungs Runes* – to both the Tolkien Estate and Tolkien Enterprises, due to my uncertainty as to which might be the copyright holder. This doubt proved to be prophetic, in a sense, for the issue was to cast a long shadow over the manuscript's publication prospects. Over a year later, in March 2001, a response came from Tolkien Enterprises expressing

Figure 5. Copy of the original letter received by the author from Tolkien Enterprises.

interest in 'this kind of creative project' with a promise that a member of their acquisitions team would be in touch.

Before that eventuated, however, a response also came from the Tolkien Department at HarperCollins that was far less encouraging: indeed, it was a cease-and-desist letter threatening legal action if I were to in any way develop or distribute the offending manuscript. In some perplexity I phoned the relevant editor in HarperCollins's London team and asked for an explanation of the hostile response I had received, while also mentioning the show of interest from Tolkien Enterprises.

In essence, I was told that the Tolkien Estate was 'not keen' on adaptations of this kind. The rival US Tolkien Enterprises had previously licensed a 'similar work', *The Lord of the Rings Tarot Deck and Game* by Stephen Donaldson, to an American publisher, resulting in legal action by the Estate, who argued that the text was a book, not a game, and that the rights (including the right of refusal) therefore belonged to the Estate. According to the Tolkien Department, the Estate won the case, and a sizeable number of copies of the book were pulped. I was warned that were my book to come to publication in any way, shape or form, similar action would result, including claims for legal costs. Tolkien Enterprises subsequently declined to publish the project, due to ongoing legal issues with the Estate.

While exasperating to me personally, I can see that the case is not clear-cut and that tensions are bound to exist between high priests intent on preserving the 'purity' of a canon, on the one hand, and IP merchants bent on squeezing every penny of profit from a franchise, all the way to casino slot machines. Yet it also seems to me that constraints of this kind on fan appropriation of a transmedia franchise which has also become a widely shared cultural mythology is deeply problematic and potentially destructive of creativity. Like Bilbo Baggins, the 'bourgeois burglar' of *The Hobbit* who steals his way into Gollum's lair and uplifts the cursed ring, Tolkien himself lifted the essence of the ring cycle from Norse mythology: even the name Gandalf (meaning 'staff-wielding elf') is taken from the great epic poem, *Voluspa*. Thus, Baggins may be regarded as metonymic, at what literary theorists call the meta-textual level, of J. R. R. Tolkien himself: pickpocket of the ring. It's a salutary thought that were the Old Norse mythic materials to have had their own lords of the franchise policing this ancient IP, *The Lord of the Rings* could never have been published. ●

Lords of the Franchise: *The Lord of the Rings*, IP Rights and Policing Appropriation
Paul Mountfort

~~~~~~~~~~~~~

GO FURTHER

Books

The Letters of J.R.R. Tolkien
Humphrey Carpenter
(London: HarperCollins, 2012)

Chinese Poetry and Prophecy: The Written Oracle in East Asia
Michel Strickmann
(Stanford, CA: SUP, 2005)

Nordic Runes
Paul Mountfort
(Rochester, VT: ITI, 2002)

A Tolkien Bestiary
David Day
(London: Chancellor Press, 2001)

J.R.R. Tolkien: Author of the Century
Tom Shippey
(London: HarperCollins, 2001)

The Lord of the Rings Part I: The Fellowship of the Ring
J. R. R. Tolkien
(London: HarperCollins, 1997 [1954])

Tolkien: A Celebration
Joseph Pearce (ed.)
(London: Fount, 1995)

Tolkien's Ring, Illustrated by Alan Lee
David Day
(London: HarperCollins, 1995)

Norse Poems
W. H. Auden and Paul B. Taylor
(London: Athlone Press, 1981)

Master of Middle-earth: The Achievement of J.R.R. Tolkien
Paul Kocher
(London: Thames and Hudson, 1972)

Essays/Extracts/Articles

'Tarot Guide Books as a Literary Genre'
Paul Mountfort
In Emily Auger (ed.). *Tarot in Culture*
(Clifford, ON: Valleyhome Books, 2014). E-text.

'The Names of the Runes'
E. Polomé
In Alfred Bammesberger (ed.). *Old English Runes and Their Continental Background*
(Heidelberg: Carl Winter – Universitatsverlag, 1991). E-text.

Online

'Making Sense of the latest Tolkien Lawsuit'
Douglas C. Kane
TheOneRing.net. 16 July 2013, http://www.theonering.net/torwp/2013/07/16/75725-making-sense-of-the-latest-tolkien-lawsuit/.

'My Father's "Eviscerated" Work: Son of Hobbit Scribe J.R.R. Tolkien Finally Speaks Out'
Raphaëlle Rérolle
Worldcrunch.com. 5 December 2012, http://www.worldcrunch.com/culture-society/my-father-039-s-quot-eviscerated-quot-work-son-of-hobbit-scribe-j.r.r.-tolkien-finally-speaks-out/hobbit-silmarillion-lord-of-rings/c3s10299/#.VBIy3oC1Y98.

'Tolkien Estate Sues Warner Over Lord of the Rings Games'
Edvard Pettersson
Bloomberg.com. 20 November 2012, http://www.bloomberg.com/news/2012-11-20/tolkien-estate-sues-warner-over-lord-of-the-rings-games.html.

'Warner Bros Sued For $80M by J.R.R. Tolkien Estate and Publisher'
Dominic Pattern
Deadline.com. 19 November 2012, http://deadline.com/2012/11/warner-bros-sued-for-80m-by-j-r-r-tolkien-estate-publisher-374789/.

'Christopher Tolkien gives rare interview to French newspaper, *Le Monde*'

Lords of the Franchise: *The Lord of the Rings*, IP Rights and Policing Appropriation
Paul Mountfort

Josh Vogt
The Examiner. 12 July 2012.
http://www.examiner.com/article/christopher-tolkien-gives-rare-interview-to-french-
newspaper-le-monde

'Tolkien, l'anneau de la discorde'
Raphaëlle Rérolle
Le Monde.fr. 5 July 2012, http://www.lemonde.fr/culture/article/2012/07/05/tolkien-l-
anneau-de-la-discorde_1729858_3246.html.

'Tolkien Estate to Time Warner: Pay Up or No Hobbit Film'
Scott Thill
Wired.com. 16 July 2009, http://www.wired.com/2009/07/tolkien-estate-to-time-
warner-pay-up-or-no-hobbit-film/.

'Litigation May Threaten Hobbit Films.' *The New Zealand Herald*, 15 July 2009, http://
www.nzherald.co.nz/nz/news/article.cfm?c_id=1&objectid=10584693.

'"Hobbit" Heirs Seek $?20 Million for "Rings" Rights'
Bret Pulley
Bloomberg.com. 15 July 2009, http://www.bloomberg.com/apps/news?pid=newsarchiv
e&sid=aiAEIATGLREU.

'A Few Frequently Asked Questions...' *TolkienEstate.com* (n.d.), http://www.tolkien-
estate.com/faq/p_2/.

'Middle-earth Enterprises.' *Wikia* (n.d.), http://lotr.wikia.com/wiki/Middle-Earth_Enter-
prises.

'Tolkien Estate Obtains Subpoena Against eSnips'
http://www.marketwired.com/press-release/tolkien-estate-obtains-subpoena-
against-esnips-636841.htm

Websites

'Tolkien Estate.' *Wikipedia*: http://en.wikipedia.org/wiki/Tolkien_Estate.

"THE *LORD OF THE RINGS* FILMS ARE NOT MADE FOR OSCARS, THEY ARE MADE FOR THE AUDIENCE."

PETER JACKSON

Chapter
09

Writing the Star: _The Lord of the Rings_ and the Production of Star Narratives

Anna Martin

→ The media promotion of the *Lord of the Rings* trilogy synergized three distinct technological and cultural developments of the early twenty-first century. The combination of DVD technology, the expansion of broadband Internet and user-based content, and the development of celebrity culture as we know it today resulted in the evolution of a new model of star marketing, based more on familiarity and intimacy than was previously the norm. This chapter will look in particular at the marketing of the *Lord of the Rings* star Viggo Mortensen in this context.

The development of DVD technology allowed the packaging of behind-the-scenes material along with feature films. James Cameron and George Lucas had already exploited this capacity in DVD releases of *Titanic* (1997) and the *Star Wars* prequel trilogy (1999, 2002, 2005) respectively. Like *The Lord of the Rings*, these were both digital effects-heavy productions and the behind-the-scenes material was largely focused on the process of developing effects-heavy cinematography. It also focused on the challenges faced by the stars of the respective movies as they filmed in green screen studios or, in the case of *Titanic*, in cold water. The hardship suffered by stars in the filming of certain scenes is a theme that emerges throughout the *Lord of the Rings* DVD extras.

Prior to and around the release of the films, broadband Internet was expanding, and user-based content was developing as users connected with each other on message boards and user-built websites. Sites developed by fans such as *Ain't It Cool News* and *TheOneRing.net* shared information regarding the production of the trilogy. This 'unofficial campaign', as Kristin Thompson calls it in her book on the production of the trilogy, *The Frodo Franchise* (2007), 'taught Hollywood much about how fans could promote a blockbuster' (135). The use of the Internet by both producers and fans to discuss and promote the film fuelled fan interest and allowed fans to feel more involved with the production of the trilogy.

The *Lord of the Rings* trilogy was released at a time when celebrity culture as we know it today was beginning to emerge. Online gossip columns and newsletters were developed, such as *Popbitch* and Ted Casablanca's *The Awful Truth*. Gossip and information on the lives of stars and celebrities became more and more available, far more so than in an economy of paper magazines. This further fuelled interest in the daily lives and love lives of celebrities and stars. The bonus material included in the *Lord of the Rings* DVD box sets, particularly the extended edition box sets, capitalized on this interest. They included several featurettes on the stars of the trilogy, including *The Fellowship of the Cast* and *A Day in the Life of a Hobbit*. These DVD extras were called the 'Appendices', recalling the Appendices Tolkien included with the book trilogy. In these featurettes focusing on the stars' experiences of filming the trilogy, the 'Appendices' devoted a lot of time to interviews and behind-the-scenes footage, with commentary from the cast on set. They focused on intimacy and familiarity with and between the stars. In interviews, stars told anecdotes about incidents during filming, which allowed fans to feel privy to the personal experience of making the movies. These insights, however, were not inert, simple reflections on the process and experience of filming. They resulted in the production of the star images of a cast that was largely unknown prior to the release of the trilogy. The production and marketing of star images has been standard practice since the early days of Hollywood. Theorists such as Richard Dyer have noted that the marketing of movies and movie stars is intertwined and mutually dependent. The fact that so few of the core cast of the film were established stars at the time of release allowed the producers of *The Lord of the Rings* significant scope for the production and

Writing the Star: *The Lord of the Rings* and the Production of Star Narratives
Anna Martin

development of the stars of the trilogy. The 'Appendices' in the extended edition DVDs were central to the production and marketing of these stars.

The beginnings of what we now recognize as celebrity culture, the development of DVD technology, and the expansion of broadband Internet and user-generated content came together in the production of the trilogy's star images. This chapter will suggest that the promotional material featuring the stars of the trilogy produced star images in specific ways, ways that invited fans' active engagement with the production of star narratives.

The star image and transmedia narratives

In this chapter, I am taking Richard Dyer's approach to reading the star. In his seminal work *Stars* (1979; revised edition 1998), Dyer argues that the star is an image made up of the myriad of articles, photos, videos, interviews and of course movies, that feature the star. The star image is so widely disseminated, fractured across so many different media – TV shows, interview spots, feature articles, movies, advertisements, and so on – that the image can never cohere into one 'true' image. The polysemy of the star image and the excess of meaning embodied by the star allow for various and potentially contradictory understandings of the star image. Because it is disseminated across so many media platforms, the star image through time can be understood as a transmedia narrative.

Fan theorist Henry Jenkins identifies the time of the release of the *Lord of the Rings* trilogy, the early 2000s, as a key period in the development of transmedia narratives. It was at this time that *The Matrix Trilogy* (Larry Wachowski and Lana Wachowski, 1999, 2003, 2003) asked viewers to follow the narrative across several platforms, including film, video games and graphic novels. In online conversation, these viewers then discussed various plot points and narrative clues and so, working collaboratively, they experienced a richer narrative than viewers who watched the movies outside of this collaborative context. *The Matrix Trilogy* was an experiment in transmedia storytelling, one that was not entirely successful. Nevertheless, it was an indication that audiences at this time were becoming interactive and collaborative online.

This idea of an interactive, collaborative community of viewers offers a model by which to understand the fan communities who participated in the fandom based on the stars of *The Lord of the Rings*. Fanfiction is fiction written by fans, usually based on a TV show or movie franchise, and usually focuses on the love lives of fictional characters. 'Real Person Fanfiction' (RPF) is based on 'real people', usually TV or movie stars or members of bands, and again most often focuses on their love and sex lives. RPF differs from fanfiction based on fictional characters insofar as there is no single, identifiable text that can be said to be the 'canon' of the fandom. Though active canons are often serial TV shows or movie franchises – and are therefore incomplete and constantly expanding and changing – they are identifiable as particular texts: the *Supernatural* fandom, for example, is based on the television show *Supernatural* (Eric Kripke, WB/CW, 2005–present), and the Marvel fandom is based on the Marvel movies and TV franchises, including *The Avengers* (Joss Whedon, 2012). RP fandoms, however, are based on texts that exist not as a single canon with identifiable parameters but rather as a collation of publicity and bonus material, usually related to a specific movie or TV project. Fans work together to collate material that collectively forms the canon. In the *Lord of the Rings* RPF fandom, this meant forming online communities where publicity photographs, interview transcripts, and other publicity material could be posted, shared and discussed. It is in this dynamic interrelationship of online artefacts and fan talk that the canon is formed. The earliest of these communities formed soon after the release of *The Fellowship of the Ring* (2001). Kristen Thompson notes that the earliest *Lord of the Rings* RPF mailing lists on *Yahoo!Groups* were founded a mere ten days after the theatrical opening of the movie.

It was the intimacy and familiarity that fans believed they had with the stars of *The Lord of the Rings* that led to the growth of the *Lord of the Rings* RPF fandom. Actor–character resonance is a central element of that sense of intimacy. Actor–character resonance is what I call the way in which stars are produced to recall and resonate with the characters they play. It describes the effect of blurring the distinction between an actor and his/her character in the publicity material related to a TV show or movie and in fanworks. The resonance fans perceive between actor and character is central to the production of star images and the production of RPF. As a case study, Viggo Mortensen provides a clear example of how exactly actor–character resonance is produced throughout the 'Appendices'. The following section details how that resonance is created, and will continue with a discussion of how the sense of intimacy effected in fans by actor–character resonance opens the star image to particular readings.

Viggo Mortensen

Viggo Mortensen, a largely unknown actor prior to the release of *The Fellowship of the Ring*, was cast very late in comparison to the rest of the actors of the Fellowship. Stuart Townsend had been cast in the role of Aragorn, but realizing he was too young, the filmmakers quickly recast. Mortensen is presented in the behind-the-scenes documentary *The Fellowship of the Cast* as the natural choice at this point. It is never mentioned that the part was initially (and repeatedly) offered to Daniel Day-Lewis. This is probably for a number of reasons, chief among them, presumably, that it would seem disrespectful to Mortensen, but also because it would disrupt the narrative that the earlier casting of Stuart Townsend was a lapse in judgement, followed by the realization that Mortensen was the natural fit for the role.

Throughout the paratexts related to the trilogy, Mortensen's narrative is thematically paralleled to that of Aragorn, culminating in a moment in which Mortensen himself is honoured as a king. *The Fellowship of the Cast*, a featurette included in the extended edition of *The Fellowship of the Ring*, focuses on his eccentricity and strangeness as described by his castmates and Peter Jackson. Dominic Monaghan tells us that '[m]ost

Writing the Star: *The Lord of the Rings* and the Production of Star Narratives
Anna Martin

times that you're with Viggo, something amazing is never far behind. He's like an old-fashioned movie star in my eyes'. Monaghan goes on to describe Mortensen as gentlemanly and polite, 'very concentrated in his art [...] I would describe Viggo as being very inspiring'. 'You can see the wildness in his eyes,' says Wood. 'He goes slightly mental.' Sean Bean tells us that '[h]e's an extraordinary guy, really. I mean, he believes in the truth of everything he does, I think, no matter what it is. And if he doesn't, he doesn't do it.' Viggo is an artist; 'an incredible artist in so many different forms,' says Monaghan. 'Photography and painting and poetry,' continues Bean. 'And he just lives for the moment, it seems. He lives for life.' The documentary reproduces some of Mortensen's photography, specifically photographs of the cast of the trilogy that he has taken during production. Liv Tyler tells the story of the make-up bus which, during the progress of principal photography, Mortensen covered in a collage of photographs he had taken.

'He doesn't just act the character,' says Jackson. 'He has to somehow become part of the character; he and the character have to blend.' Mortensen, according to Jackson, saw his sword as central to the character of Aragorn. He brought his sword with him wherever he went, whether on set or driving in his car or going to restaurants. 'I was on the way out of a Sunday rehearsal,' says Mortensen,

> and I was walking out of the gym, all sort of sweaty, half in street clothes and half in Aragorn clothes, waving a sword around, trying to keep a mental picture of what we'd just done. So I was walking down the street, down to where my car was parked, on a Sunday afternoon, and waving the sword around, you know, looking like this desperate Rasputin character to them [people in the area], probably. And cop-cars converged on me. There'd been some report. (Mortensen, *The Fellowship of the Cast*)

This story, in which Mortensen is 'half in street clothes and half in Aragorn clothes,' adds to the general picture developing in the viewer's mind of Mortensen as an eccentric, charismatic figure, extremely dedicated to his role. That dedication is characterized as so strong that Aragorn and Mortensen seem to blend into one. This offers the viewer a way into Mortensen's star persona, a connection with him via Aragorn. With this connection made, the viewer is invited to engage with Mortensen himself.

In the 'Appendices' included with *The Two Towers* (2002), Mortensen's dedication as an actor is a central facet of his characterization, this time in the context of pain and

Figure 1: Mortensen's first scene as the enigmatic Strider © New Line Cinema, 2001.

Figure 2: Mortensen kicks an orc helmet, breaks his toe, and cries out in pain © New Line Cinema, 2002.

endurance. 'He doesn't do the pain thing,' says Billy Boyd. 'He doesn't seem to acknowledge it' (*Warriors of the Third Age*, 'Appendices', Part 4). The documentary *Cameras in Middle-earth* ('Appendices', Part 4) includes a story about the filming of a scene in which Aragorn, thinking Merry and Pippin dead, kicks an orc helmet and then expresses his frustration and grief by crying out. In the final take, Mortensen breaks his toe kicking the helmet, and transforms his physical pain into a gut-wrenching howl of emotional pain at the loss of Merry and Pippin. This is the take that ends up in the movie.

Later in the same documentary, a member of the stunt team says,

> If I was going into battle and I needed someone to be at my right shoulder, it would be Viggo, because he just gave everything. [...] All his hands, the knuckles had chunks out of it [sic] from his sword-fighting. (*Cameras in Middle-earth*, 'Appendices', Part 4)

At one point, Mortensen broke a tooth while shooting a scene. He was prepared to superglue his tooth back in and had to be persuaded to go to the dentist. Once the tooth was repaired, he went straight back to work. Another story relates how Mortensen wanted to float down the river as Aragorn rather than allow a stuntman to do the shot. This resulted in him hitting a rock and going under the water until he managed to kick himself free. 'It was really scary,' he says, 'but the doing of it was interesting' (*Cameras in Middle-earth*, 'Appendices', Part 4).

By the time we reach the 'Appendices' included with *The Return of the King* (2003), it is Mortensen's charisma and natural leadership that emerge as the primary themes in his characterization. Perhaps the most compelling moment consolidating Mortensen's role as leader among the cast members, as well as many of the crew and stunt team, is

Writing the Star: *The Lord of the Rings* and the Production of Star Narratives
Anna Martin

the occasion upon which the stunt team performs the *haka* for Mortensen and Bernard Hill. 'Standing in front of us, we have two kings,' says Shane Rangi, the stunt performer leading the introduction. Another member of the stunt team tells us that '[t]his is only performed for dignitaries or people of importance, and, you know, Viggo, throughout the whole filming of it was really an important part of the film. He ended up being king' (*Cameras in Middle-earth*, 'Appendices', Part 6). Both Mortensen and Hill seem cognisant of the honour the stunt team are according them. The camera finds Mortensen's face in particular as he watches the stunt team perform the *haka* and he appears quite emotional.

The poster for *Return of the King* that features Aragorn reflects the doubling of character and actor, of movie star and king: the poster is a close-up of a face that belongs to both Aragorn and Mortensen at one and the same time. In the context of the story of the trilogy, the face is that of Aragorn, now taking his place as King of Gondor and holding Andúril in his hands. As an image on a movie poster, the face is Mortensen's, now a movie star with the star power to attract an audience to a major blockbuster movie.

The progression in the promotional material for the movies, then, follows Aragorn from the mysterious Strider to Aragorn, King of Gondor, while, in parallel, Mortensen's star image is developed from relatively unknown actor to major movie star. As well as that, upon watching the trilogy, these stories and moments echo through Mortensen's scenes. When Aragorn kicks the helmet and screams, the viewer now sees the diegetic action and *also* the 'behind the scenes' action, i.e. the breaking of Mortensen's toe and the physical pain that fuels his scream. When Aragorn floats down the river, the viewer is reminded of the near-drowning Mortensen suffered. These real pains and perils reverberate with the fictional events and fill the narrative with an extra layer of meaning. When Aragorn becomes king, we know that Mortensen, too, is a king of sorts on set. It works the other way, too: the cuts, injuries and dangers suffered by Mortensen also take on a greater meaning in their association with Aragorn. This is what Jonathan Gray calls the 'stacking' of the films with 'mythic resonance' (242). The stories enrich each other and invite the viewer into a double engagement: with the story of the trilogy itself and with the narrative of the production of the films.

There is a distinct sense of intimacy in this manner of producing a star. Through anecdotes and stories and personal interviews, viewers feel they get to know the 'real person' behind the star persona. The entire narrative of the making of the trilogy takes place in a bubble of intimacy, one on which the stars reflect with fondness and nostalgia. This sense of intimacy is what inspires RPF. Intimacy, in the behind-the-scenes features packaged in the DVD box sets, becomes a commodity. We are sold the intimacy of the group of stars themselves, and, in turn, our intimacy with that intimacy. As such, intimacy here is a product, not an uncomplicated engagement with the stars. The convergence of this model of stardom that stresses intimacy, the production and consumption of transmedia narratives, and the technologies upon which to deliver and reproduce these narratives produced more intensive and immersive marketing and

publicity opportunities for blockbuster movies. RPF reflects these new developments in the marketing of movie stars.

Prosuming the star image

The active audiences which constitute fandoms are sometimes referred to as 'prosumers', a neologism which refers to consumers who produce their own transformative works based on a media text. The Real Person fans who produced fanworks based on the stars of the trilogy are among the prosumers of *The Lord of the Rings*. The mode of star production employed by the producers of *The Lord of the Rings* requires a high level of prosumption. The narratives produced by the behind-the-scenes material are designed to actively engage fans' imagination. In that active engagement, fans come to feel that they know the 'real people' behind the star personae; that, in becoming familiar with the intimacy shared by the stars, they in turn share that intimacy. RPF reproduces this sense of intimacy in its stories of love between the stars. Fanfiction in general has a reputation for being preoccupied with love and sex, and RPF is almost exclusively concerned with such stories. In the context of the *Lord of the Rings* RPF, the stories are usually homoerotic in nature. As such, they reveal the homoerotics of a cast almost entirely made up of men. Fans' reading of homosocial bonds as homoerotic or homosexual challenges the 'discontinuous relation of male homosocial and homosexual bonds' identified in modern western culture by Eve Kosofsky Sedgwick (5). It insists on the *possibility* of homosexuality among the stars of a Hollywood blockbuster. Thus the work of fans in producing star narratives demonstrates the potential to read star images subversively, in ways unaligned with the dominant culture of homosocial masculinity. These narratives are produced by fans who are following transmedia narratives and remediating the star images they consume. Star images are available to such intimate fan readings thanks to New Media's promise of intimacy with the stars.

Because it was largely about men, *Lord of the Rings* RPF is more commonly known as Real Person Slash (slash being the fanfiction descriptor for stories featuring male/male relationships). The fandom was known as LOTRPS, pronounced (and sometimes written) 'Lotrips'. In the fanfiction, Mortensen is most often paired up with either Sean Bean or Orlando Bloom, as fans understood from the publicity material that these were the stars he was closest to on set and during publicity.

LOTRPS stories often recall incidents recounted in interviews. One well-known incident is Orlando Bloom's description of crossing a river with Mortensen at night. Bloom told the story in an interview, and it brings together Mortensen's love of nature, his enthusiasm for experiences in natural settings, and the sense of intimacy that exists between Bloom and Mortensen in the *Lord of the Rings* publicity material. Bloom's

Writing the Star: *The Lord of the Rings* and the Production of Star Narratives
Anna Martin

telling of the story ends with him saying, 'I can't believe how much this is going to make it sound like I'm in love with the guy.' RPS fans agreed, and produced stories about the incident in which Bloom is indeed in love with Mortensen. I call this kind of story a 'behind the public moment' story, as fans imagine the possibilities behind certain visible moments that occur in public photographs, videos, anecdotes or interviews. 'Behind the public moment' stories are very popular in all kinds of RPF, and they situate public moments in longer narratives of love and desire. These stories are indicative of the ways in which fans respond to the invitation implicit in the behind-the-scenes material to engage imaginatively, actively and intimately with star narratives.

Conclusion
In marketing intimacy as a commodity, the producers invited fans to imagine the intimate lives of the stars of the trilogy. RPF fans responded to that invitation, and as such serve as a case study in a broader analysis of the response of fans to this marketing strategy and the results of such a strategy. The remediation of the star image by fans strongly suggests that the production of stars is a collaborative project. The star narrative requires the engagement of fans if it is to have any traction; if, that is, a star is to become more and more marketable. That engagement need not take the form of RPF. In fact, RPF is just one example of a much broader trend of fascination with the lives and loves of stars. Narrative is central to stardom, and as we can see in the case of *The Lord of the Rings*, star narratives are collaboratively produced by producers, media outlets and fans. ●

~~~~~~~~~~~~~

GO FURTHER

Books

Fic: Why Fanfiction is Taking Over the World
Anne Jamison (ed.)
(Dallas, TX: BenBella Books, Inc., 2013)

The Frodo Franchise: 'The Lord of the Rings' and Modern Hollywood
Kristin Thompson
(Berkeley: University of California Press, 2007)

Convergence Culture: Where Old and New Media Collide
Henry Jenkins
(New York: NYUP, 2006)

Fan Fiction and Fan Communities in the Age of the Internet
Karen Hellekson and Kristina Busse (eds)
(Jefferson, NC: McFarland & Company, Inc., 2006)

Stars
Richard Dyer
(London: British Film Institute, 1998)

Between Men: English Literature and Male Homosocial Desire
Eve Kosofsky Sedgwick
(New York: Columbia University Press, 1985)

Extracts/Essays/Articles

'Bonus Material: The DVD Layering of *The Lord of the Rings*'
Jonathan Gray
In Ernest Mathijs (ed.). *'The Lord of the Rings': Popular Culture in a Global Context*
(London: Wallflower, 2006), pp. 262–82.

'Framing Tolkien: Trailers, High Concept and the Ring'
Erik Hedling
In Ernest Mathijs (ed.). *'The Lord of the Rings': Popular Culture in a Global Context*
(London: Wallflower, 2006), pp. 225–37.

Online

'The Hero Returns'
Tom Roston interview with Viggo Mortensen (*Premiere*, January 2003)
Reproduced at *Viggo-Works.com*, http://www.viggo-works.com/?page=87.

Chapter
10

Understanding Fans' 'Precious': The Impact of the Lord of the Rings Films on the Hobbit Movies

Abigail G. Scheg

→ The three films of Peter Jackson's *Lord of the Rings* (*LOTR*) trilogy were nominated for a total of 30 Academy Awards, and won seventeen. Specifically, *The Fellowship of the Ring* (2001) was nominated for thirteen, and won four (Cinematography, Make-up, Music – Original Score and Visual Effects), *The Two Towers* (2002) was nominated for six, and won two (Sound Editing and Visual Effects);

Figure 1: The dwarves and Bilbo Baggins (the hobbit) © 2012, Warner Brothers.

The Return of the King (2003) was nominated for and won eleven (Art Direction, Cinematography, Costume Design, Directing, Film Editing, Make-up, Music – Original Score, Music – Original Song, Best Picture, Sound Editing, Sound Mixing, Supporting Actor, Visual Effects and Adapted Screenplay) (IMDb). In addition to these Academy Awards, the *LOTR* trilogy also won several other types of awards, grossed a tremendous amount around the world in their opening weekends, and received generally favourable reviews from critics and audiences alike. Eleven years following the release of *The Fellowship of the Ring*, Peter Jackson's three-part film adaptation of *The Hobbit* hit the theatres. *The Hobbit: An Unexpected Journey* (2012), *The Hobbit: The Desolation of Smaug* (2013) and *The Hobbit: The Battle of the Five Armies* (2014) again transferred Tolkien's world to the big screen.

Unlike *The Lord of the Rings*, which was already a trilogy in print, the *Hobbit* movie trilogy was created from a single text. According to Peter Jackson, during *The Hobbit: The Desolation of Smaug* press day, it was necessary to split *The Hobbit* into three movies so that the audience was able to relate to the characters and know more of their backgrounds. In an article by *Hypable* pertaining to this press day, 'The need to be able to tell a real story and put it on par with *The Lord of the Rings* trilogy was what drove Jackson and his team to expand the world.' It is certainly understandable that Jackson would want to have success with *The Hobbit* on par, or better than, the success of *The Lord of the Rings*. However, this chapter asserts that it was the rampant success of the *Lord of the Rings* movies which made it impossible for *The Hobbit* to be as successful a film endeavour.

Understanding Fans' 'Precious':
The Impact of the Lord of the Rings Films on the Hobbit Movies
Abigail G. Scheg

According to an article by Peter Sciretta entitled, 'Peter Jackson Explains Why He's Shooting "The Hobbit" at 48 Frames Per Second' (2011), *The Hobbit* was filmed in 48 fps (frames per second), whereas the typical movie is shot at 24 fps. Sciretta's article includes excerpts from Peter Jackson's Facebook-page updates regarding the development and filming of the *Hobbit* movies, 'Shooting and projecting at 48 fps [...] looks much more lifelike, and it is much easier to watch, especially in 3-D.' Jackson further explains that movie-goers

> have lived with 24 fps for 9 decades – not because it's the best film speed (it's not by any stretch), but because it was the cheapest speed to achieve basic acceptable results back in 1927 or whenever it was adopted.

The *LOTR* series was filmed in the typical 24 fps, which means that the look of the characters, the setting, the scenes and the actions of the *Hobbit* films were significantly different to movie-goers than what they had watched not only in their previous Tolkien adaptations, but in all movies that they had ever viewed.

Some movie critics praised the way that the 48 fps film looked, whereas others found it challenging to get used to, or found that it actually pointed to flaws in characters' make-up or setting problems. However, it was not just the unique filming style that garnered attention and conversation from movie-goers.

As the *Hobbit* film series was filmed *after* the *LOTR* series, one of the challenges that film-makers had to work with was to make sure that the characters looked an appropriate age from the way that they were depicted in *LOTR*. This proved especially problematic for the character, Legolas, played by Orlando Bloom. Film-makers tried to make Legolas look younger by pulling the skin of his face taut, and through the help of CGI. With the increased film speed, all of the nuances of characters and action are under much closer scrutiny by viewers. In some parts of the film series, Legolas is just difficult to look at. He looks like a fuzzy caricature of Orlando Bloom – maybe Orlando Bloom meets the Ghost of Christmas Past from *The Muppet Christmas Carol* (Brain Henson,

Figure 3: Tauriel (played by
Evangeline Lilly) and Legolas
(played by Orlando Bloom)
©2013, Warner Brothers.

1992). Legolas's presentation was both distracting and disappointing to viewers, as he was one of the major, popular characters of the *LOTR* movies, and one that audiences were looking forward to seeing again in the *Hobbit* series.

The film style became increasingly problematic as the series continued, and was especially problematic in the third film. Most notably, there is a scene where Legolas jumps from falling rock to falling rock as a stone bridge collapses. This scene, in particular, received a tremendous amount of negative feedback from viewers. Part of the negative feedback was for the sheer unbelieveability of this scene; Legolas, while an impressive character in both the *LOTR* books and movies, does not possess the ability to fly, and shouldn't be depicted as a character with this type of 'super human' strength, even for one of the most notable elves in the films. The feedback was also negative because of the way that this scene actually looked on the screen; viewers were not able to suspend reality *that much* for this film and the characters. Though these movies are based on fictional texts, one of the significant charms of Tolkien's stories was that he did create a thorough and well-rounded world. There were hobbits and elves, and a sense of accuracy, rules and behaviours. Legolas's rock-jumping capabilities did not fit in with the characterization, or the root novels of Tolkien's texts.

The unique challenge of creating the *LOTR* and *Hobbit* film adaptations are that there are source texts to serve as background for these movies. Long have movies been criticized for departing from their source material, and sometimes the relation or deviation from the source material can make or break the audiences' relationship and investment in a film. Bertha Chin and Jonathan Gray's article 'One Ring to Rule Them All: Pre-viewers and Pre-texts of the *Lord of the Rings*' sought to evaluate how audiences evaluated the *LOTR* movies before they were even created. By analysing online discussion board postings, these researchers found that all postings came from

Understanding Fans''Precious':
The Impact of the Lord of the Rings Films on the Hobbit Movies
Abigail G. Scheg

individuals who loved the *LOTR* texts. Chin and Gray found that there were generally three categories of positions represented: 'those who are inclined to dislike the films, those who are inclined to love them, and those who balance themselves somewhere in between' (online). The first category, 'those who are inclined to dislike the films,' feel strongly connected to the books, and, as they are described in the article, feel that 'the story *is* the books' (Chin and Gray), and no film adaptation would do justice to the story. This phenomenon is true of any book-to-movie transformation; audiences are both intrigued, and appalled, by changes from the original text to the big screen. Chin and Gray refer to this as 'textual purism', stating that this position is generally rare, 'More common is a negotiated, balanced position, whereby Tolkien fans hope for three great films, and are willing to allow the film-makers some leeway in transferring the books to screen, but nevertheless remain somewhat fearful.' As stated previously, one of the great charms of Tolkien's stories is his creation of a holistic world, much like that of J. K. Rowling's *Harry Potter* series (1997-2007). Rowling, like Tolkien, created an entire magical world that held its own boundaries and rules, whether explicitly stated, or implied by author and understood by the audience. Audiences tend to allow slight latitude in the transformation of a written text to the big screen, but *The Hobbit* stretched the text's boundaries and rules.

The final category of individuals are 'those who are inclined to love them', finding the film adaptations to be extensions of the text stories, and therefore, entertaining regardless of the precision of presentation. Since the *Hobbit* trilogy had not only the challenges of relating to and creating an agreeable film for the textual purists, but also to align itself with the success and fandom of the *LOTR* movies, the *Hobbit* films were generated with quite a weight of preconceived notion. Some audience members just want to love the *LOTR* and likewise the *Hobbit* trilogies because they are pleased to see these stories and characters take on a new life, and take on new meaning for a younger generation of readers and viewers. An additional challenge of movies based on texts is that the audience sometimes makes these decisions as to whether the movie is 'good' before they have even seen it.

In the article 'Framing Audience Prefigurations of *The Hobbit: An Unexpected Journey*: The Roles of Fandom, Politics and Idealized Intertexts', authors Charles H. Davis, Carolyn Michelle, Ann Hardy and Craig Hight assert that 'Audiences for blockbuster event-films sequels and adaptations often formulate highly developed expectations, motivations, understandings, and opinions well before the films are released' (50). In particular, these authors found that the *Hobbit* films faced a number of pre-conceived evaluations from audiences based on the text and the success of the *LOTR* films. In particular, these authors identified the following: 'Notably, some sought a familiar look and feel from Jackson's earlier *Lord of the Rings* film trilogy, while others required fidelity, credibility, and a compelling interpretation in the *Hobbit* book-to-film screen adaptation' (58). Admittedly, I was one of the viewers who based my willingness to see the

Figure 4: Smaug and Bilbo Baggins © 2013, Warner Brothers.

Hobbit films on my love for the *LOTR* films. As a viewer, I wanted to be immersed in Middle-earth again, and, even unbeknownst to myself, I had high expectations of the *Hobbit* films because of their film predecessors. The authors continue,

> Furthermore, as an intended global blockbuster, the film also sought audiences beyond its acquired fan base. In a widening circle, *The Hobbit*'s addressee audiences included younger males with an interest in action adventure and special effects films, families with children, individuals interested in one or another of the actors in *The Hobbit*, and casual holiday-period movie-goers (58).

Therefore, not only did Jackson's *The Hobbit* face the challenges of appeasing an audience as in a normal text-to-film adaptation, but it also faced challenges with alignment to a pre-conceived (and growing) audience, film aficionados, and the large fan base of the *LOTR* films. Typically, movies already have the pressure of wanting to attract fans and a large viewership imposed upon them. However, with the added pressure of textual pureism, among other things, it seems that *The Hobbit*, though monetarily successful in the theatres, never truly stood a chance with audiences.

Films are typically split into specific audience groups, ratings and genres for the purposes of advertising and marketing to a target audience. Although specifics of genre classification can vary based on elements of the film such as the actors or the setting, the marketing processes for movie releases typically have a very narrow audience scope to which they are advertising and trying to appeal. As Charles H. Davis, Carolyn Michelle, Ann Hardy and Craig Hight indicated in the quotes in the previous paragraph, the *LOTR* series proved to be effective at targeting a large body of interested movie-goers spanning age groups and other demographics. The fan base for the *LOTR* films only increased over the development and release of the latter films. As an indication, according to IMDb, *The Fellowship of the Ring* opened in the United States with $47,211,490, as compared to the opening of *The Return of the King* (2003), which opened in the United States with $72,629,713. Likewise, then, this expectation of continued success extended to the *Hobbit* series. The expectation was that the fan base would only continue to grow, but this expectation was based on the success of *LOTR*, not on the individual development of *The Hobbit* itself. This pattern of expectation of *The Hobbit* films based on the *LOTR* film series can also be seen when examining critical reviews of the films.

Roger Ebert's 2001 review of *The Fellowship of the Ring* explains that Ebert had to return to Tolkien's novel itself to remember the draw of the story, and the presentation of the details. In revisiting the novel, he found a fantasy world aptly captured by Jackson's film,

Understanding Fans' 'Precious':
The Impact of the Lord of the Rings Films on the Hobbit Movies
Abigail G. Scheg

Figure 5: Battle preparation
in The Hobbit: Battle of the
Five Armies © 2014, Warner
Brothers,

Peter Jackson, the New Zealand director who masterminded this film [...] has made a work for, and of, our times. It will be embraced, I suspect, by many Tolkien fans and take on aspects of a cult. It is a candidate for many Oscars. It is an awesome production in its daring and breadth, and there are many small touches that are just right.

Ebert's review of the film proved to be accurate in terms of fan base and candidacy for awards. Sheila O'Malley's 2013 review (from Roger Ebert's website) on *The Hobbit: The Desolation of Smaug* opens with the Tolkien quote, 'Fantasy (in this sense) is, I think, not a lower but a higher form of Art, indeed the most nearly pure form, and so (when achieved) the most potent.' Then, her review begins by stating that she 'did not find that quality in *An Unexpected Journey*.' O'Malley praises the further development and depiction of Middle-earth as 'breathtaking', but repeatedly criticizes the unnecessary length of scenes. For instance, the scenes with Smaug are very limited in the text, but in the movies, Smaug has a starring role (particularly in the second film), and very lengthy monologues that do not move the plot along. Viewers become trapped in these lengthy scenes, unable to escape them, searching for meaning in the development of the plot, but finding nothing to make it worth their while.

David Blaustein's review, entitled 'Movie Review: *The Hobbit: An Unexpected Journey* Not as Good as *Lord of the Rings*' (2012), echoes this concern and appropriately summarizes his perspective on the *Hobbit* films as they relate to the *LOTR* series. In asking, 'what's wrong with *The Hobbit: An Unexpected Journey*,' Blaustein answers,

Thankfully, not much, except for the pacing for the first hour – an hour that's simultaneously exhilarating and frustrating in its attention to detail in both story and aesthetic. Jackson and company just try to do a little too much of everything, including 3D. Understandably, those who want to see every little detail of the book come to life (and then some) will get exactly what they want, but if you'd rather not sit in a movie theatre for three hours, then it's not necessary.

Likewise, a review from Mick LaSalle entitled '*The Hobbit* Review: Chore of the Rings' (2012), criticizes the length of the movie, as well as the decision to split *The Hobbit* into three films. He asserts, 'This puts a lot of pressure on a simple story [...] This pressure, this obligation to stretch everything to the limits of endurance and beyond, is felt from the film's early minutes.' While the *LOTR* films were appropriately split into three films, audiences expected the depiction of plot and characters in the *Hobbit* films to match the intensity and pace of the *LOTR* films. Therefore, though the presentation of Middle-earth in the *Hobbit* films was beautiful, the pace of the films does not hold audiences' attention or interest like that of the *LOTR* films.

LOTR had many characters' storylines running simultaneously, and the film gracefully moved back and forth between characters and locations with a steady increase in the action and intensity throughout the trilogy. Because the *Hobbit* film series is only based on a single text, without as many scenes and characters to move between, the films became tedious to watch. The bulk of the characters of the *Hobbit* series are the dwarves (plus Bilbo), who congregate together for the majority of the films. The scenes and the films of the *Hobbit* series themselves, were far longer than they needed to be to tell the story and show the adventure of the text. Likewise, the *Hobbit* text is focused mostly on the character of the hobbit, Bilbo Baggins, but the film, as a trilogy, takes the focus off of the hobbit without a clear focus on what the remainder of the screen-time should focus upon. Perhaps, as other movie critics indicate, the focus is on the relationship between Peter Jackson, Tolkien and the entertainment quality of film-making.

Peter Bradshaw's review from *The Guardian*, 'The Hobbit: The Desolation of Smaug Review' (2013), has the notable tagline: 'Finally I get it! The fuss isn't just about Tolkien, it's about Peter Jackson and Tolkien – and they are hugely enjoyable together.' Bradshaw's review does not singularly address *The Hobbit: The Desolation of Smaug* as a single film, nor does he solely relate it to its direct predecessor, *The Hobbit: An Unexpected Journey*, but rather, he contextualizes it within the conversation of all of Peter Jackson's Tolkien films, including the entire *LOTR* series. He explains, 'in fact I came to the *Lord of the Rings: The Fellowship of the Ring* in 2001 with some unbelief,' but then, 'With the Hobbit series, the penny is properly dropping: it's not about Tolkien, it's Tolkien-plus-Jackson, of course. It's morphed into something new.' Bradshaw's review, therefore, does not make the argument that *The Hobbit: The Desolation of Smaug* is an enjoyable single film, but rather it is part of an ongoing epic adventure of a high calibre. Tolkien-plus-Jackson, as he indicates, has developed into its own genre of film-making which comes with great expectation from the audience that somehow all of the elements, and all of the characters, will come together in a beautiful and graceful execution.

The challenges that besieged the *Hobbit* films were significant before the first film was even created or released. The unique experience of developing a prequel series after releasing a film series presents problems on a variety of levels for the director, the actors and all the individuals associated with the creation of the film. The *Hobbit* series will undoubtedly become a classic movie series, praised by movie lovers, Tolkien aficionados and *LOTR* fans. With the differentiation of the *Hobbit* from the *LOTR* series, movie-goers need to reflect upon the uniqueness of this series, as well as its alignment

Understanding Fans' 'Precious':
The Impact of the Lord of the Rings Films on the Hobbit Movies
Abigail G. Scheg

with, what Bradshaw indicated as, the Tolkien-plus-Jackson genre. In this reflection, fans will ultimately find themselves recognizing the *Hobbit* series as another one of their precious films. ●

~~~~~~~~~~~~~~~~

GO FURTHER

Extracts/Essays/Articles

Framing Audience Prefigurations of *The Hobbit: An Unexpected Journey:* The Roles of Fandom, Politics and Idealized Intertexts
Charles H. Davis, Carolyn Michelle, Ann Hardy and Craig Hight
In *Participations: Journal of Audience & Reception Studies.* 11:1 (2004), pp. 50-87.

'One Ring to Rule Them All': Pre-viewers and Pre-texts of the *Lord of the Rings*'
Bertha Chin and Jonathan Gray
In *Intensities: The Journal of Cult Media.* 2:2 (2002). Online.

Online

'*The Hobbit: The Desolation of Smaug*' [Review]
Sheila O'Malley
RogerEbert.com. 13 December 2013, http://www.rogerebert.com/reviews/the-hobbit-the-desolation-of-smaug-2013.

'*The Hobbit: The Desolation of Smaug* Review'
Peter Bradshaw
The Guardian. 12 December 2013, http://www.theguardian.com/film/2013/dec/12/.hobbit-desolation-of-smaug-review.

'Peter Jackson Explains Why *The Hobbit* Has to Be Three Movies'
Andrew Sims
Hypable. 11 December 2013, http://www.hypable.com/2013/12/11/why-is-hobbit-three-movies-peter-jackson/.

'*The Hobbit* Review: Chore of the Rings'
Mick LaSalle
Sfgate.com. 13 December 2012, http://www.sfgate.com/movies/article/The-Hobbit-review-Chore-of-the-Rings-4116150.php.

'Movie Review: *The Hobbit: An Unexpected Journey* Not as Good as *Lord of the Rings*'
David Blaustein
ABC News. 13 December 2012,
 http://abcnews.go.com/blogs/entertainment/2012/12/movie-review-the-hobbit.

'Peter Jackson Explains Why He's Shooting *The Hobbit* at 48 Frames Per Second'
Peter Sciretta
SlashFilm.com. 11 April 2011, http://www.slashfilm.com/peter-jackson-explains-shoot-ing-the-hobbit-48-frames/.

'*Lord of the Rings: The Fellowship of the Ring*' [Review]
RogerEbert.com. 19 December 2001,
http://www.rogerebert.com/reviews/lord-of-the-rings-the-fellowship-of-the-ring-2001.

Websites

'*The Lord of the Rings: The Fellowship of the Ring* 2001' | 'Awards', International Movie
Database (IMDb): http://www.imdb.com/title/tt0120737/awards?ref_=tt_ql_4.

'*The Lord of the Rings: The Return of the King* 2003' | 'Box office': International Movie
Database (IMDb), http://www.imdb.com/title/tt0167260/business?ref_=tt_dt_bus.

Contributor Details

EDITOR

Lorna Piatti-Farnell, PhD, is Director of the Popular Culture Research Centre at Auckland University of Technology, New Zealand. Her research interest focus mainly on interdisciplinary perspectives on contemporary popular culture – film and literature in particular –and lie at the intersection of Gothic studies, cultural history, food studies, and participatory cultures. Lorna is President of the Gothic Association of New Zealand and Australia, and Chair of Gothic and Horror for the Popular Culture Association of Australia and New Zealand. She has written three monographs to date: *The Vampire in Contemporary Popular Literature* (2014), *Beef: A Global History* (2013) and *Food and Culture in Contemporary American Fiction* (2011). Lorna is currently working on a new monograph, entitled *Consuming Gothic: Food and Horror in Contemporary Film*, to be published by Palgrave.

CONTRIBUTORS

Cait Coker is an Associate Editor for *Foundation: The International Review of Science Fiction*. Her research focuses on the depictions of women and sexuality in science fiction and fantasy.

Emily Gray, PhD, hails from Walsall, UK and is currently a lecturer in Education Studies at RMIT University in Melbourne, Australia. Her publications include refereed journal articles, book chapters, and an edited collection entitled *Queer Teachers, Identity and Performativity* co-edited with Anne Harris. Emily's theoretical interests are interdisciplinary and she draws from the fields of sociology, cultural studies and education primarily to consider questions of how attempts to teach social justice issues are both enabled and constrained within different pedagogical settings. Emily's work also explores popular culture, public pedagogies and audience studies and she considers how popular culture is deployed as a pedagogical tool and with the effects that this produces.

Anna Martin, PhD, completed undergraduate and Masters level studies at Trinity College, Dublin, and received her PhD from Lancaster University, UK. Her research focuses on online fan cultures, with particular interest in the textual practices of fans. Her doctoral thesis focused on Real Person Fanfiction (RPF) and RPF communities, arguing that these communities produce polysemic narratives of both stars and fans, thereby offering an insight into the fan response to star images and marketing, as well as fannish self-positioning in relation to other fans. The RPF fandom surrounding *Lord of the Rings* was a key case study in her work. She has presented her work to positive response at several academic conferences. Currently, Anna is teaching English in Japan while continuing with her research on an independent basis.

Maggie Parke, PhD, earned her doctorate in Film and Digital Media, focusing on the adaptation processes of event films and fan management. Her research included working on set for *Twilight* (2008), *Captain America* (2009), and at Turbine Inc., the gaming company behind *Lord of the Rings* Online (LOTRO) and DC Comic's new game, *Infinite Crisis*. She currently works in both education and the film industry. She develops projects with Elfin Productions, and is a freelance script editor and consultant for fan management, and also works at Bangor University in Wales, UK. She has been published in *The Journal of Gaming and Virtual Worlds* (2009), co-edited a book of Critical Essays on *Twilight* (McMillan, 2011), writes for *Hypable*, and has a column with *PagetoPremiere. com*. She has lectured internationally at high schools and universities, and also at film festivals and fan conventions including The Hay Festival, LeakyCon, and TwiCon.

Paul Mountfort, PhD, leads the undergraduate programmes in English and New Media Studies and Creative Writing at Auckland University of Technology, New Zealand. He is the author of two full-length books on the uses of ancient letters in art, literature and transmedia, storytelling, and has been a regular speaker at the Popular/American Culture Association annual conferences. His research areas are primarily concerned with transmedia storytelling, visual language, and digital literacies.

Miguel Ángel Pérez-Gómez has a Bachelor´s Degree in Media Studies with a Major in Audiovisual Communication from the University of Seville. He is a PhD student in the Department of Media Studies, Advertising and Literature of the Faculty of Communication, University of Seville, working on a thesis on fandom and participatory cultures. He has participated in international events as *Queer Screen Cultures* at Nottingham University (2009), AATI Conferences (Italy), and *Beyond Don Juan: Rethinking Iberian Masculinities* (New York University, 2011) and recently in *Historieta o comic: biografia del fumetto in Spagna* (Universitá Ca'Foscari, Venezia). In 2011, he edited the e-book *Previously On: Multidisciplinary Studies on TV Series in the Third Golden Age of Television*. He also writes about comics in: *El lector Bicefalo, Entrecomics* and *Rock de Lux*.

Alexander Sergeant is a PhD candidate within the Department of Film Studies at King's College London. His thesis examines issues of spectatorship in relation to the Hollywood fantasy genre and was supported by a grant from the UK Arts and Humanities Research Council. His research interests include the history of Hollywood cinema, film theory, theories of film spectatorship, film philosophy and psychoanalysis. He has published on these subjects in a variety of academic journals and edited collections.

Abigail G. Scheg, PhD, is an Assistant Professor of English. She also serves as a dissertation chair for Northcentral and Grand Canyon Universities. She researches, conferences, and publishes in the areas of composition, distance education, and popular culture. She is the author or editor of six texts spanning from education, to online pedagogy, to teaching with technology, and popular culture. Her edited collection, *Bullying in Popular Culture*, was published by McFarland Publishing in 2015.

Karen Viars is a librarian and writer in Atlanta, Georgia. Her research interests include fantasy and science fiction, instructional design and teaching in academic libraries.

Joshua Wille is a Ph.D. student in Film and Media Studies at the University of Kansas, where his research is focused on fan edits and film revisionism. His writing on the theory and practice of fan editing has been published in *Transformative Works and Cultures* and in the book *Fan Phenomena: James Bond* (Intellect, 2015). As a fan editor himself, Wille created *Watchmen: Midnight* (2011), an alternative version of the film *Watchmen* (2009) that more closely reflects the narrative structure, characterizations, and spirit of the original comics by Alan Moore and Dave Gibbons. Wille has delivered research-oriented presentations along with screenings of *Watchmen: Midnight* at fan conventions and academic events in the United States, Germany, and the Netherlands.

Image Credits

From *The Lord of the Rings* trilogy
Chapter 1:   Fig.2-5 ©New Line Cinema
Chapter 3:   Fig.4 ©New Line Cinema
Chapter 9:   Fig.1-3 ©New Line Cinema

From *The Wizard of Oz*
Chapter 1:   Fig.1 ©Metro-Goldwyn-Meyer

From *Triumph of the Will*
Chapter 1:   Fig.5 ©Reichsparteitag Film

From *The Hobbit* trilogy
Chapter 10:   Fig.1-5 ©Warner Brothers

Additional images
Introduction: Fig.1 ©New Line Cinema
Introduction: Fig.2 ©Lorna Piatti-Farnell
Introduction: Fig.3 ©Hobbiton Movie Set Tours
Chapter 2:   Fig.1-5 ©Creative Commons
Chapter 3:   Fig.1 ©HAL 9000 and Phil Dragash
Chapter 3:   Fig.2-3 ©Kerr
Chapter 3:   Fig.5 ©Shannon Brownlee
Chapter 4:   Fig.2 ©Actors at Work
Chapter 4:   Fig.3 ©Independent Online Cinema
Chapter 4:   Fig.4 ©Tom Robinson Productions
Chapter 5:   Fig.1 ©Lorna Piatti-Farnell
Chapter 5:   Fig-2-5 ©Hobbiton Movie Set Tours
Chapter 6:   Fig 1-6 ©Emily Gray
Chapter 7:   Fig.1 ©Francesco Amadio
Chapter 7:   Fig.2 ©neverland300690
Chapter 7:   Fig.3 ©Suzana Uhr
Chapter 8:   Fig.1 ©ACE Publishing
Chapter 8:   Fig.2 ©The Lego Group
Chapter 8:   Fig.3 ©ZhuoKu
Chapter 8:   Fig.4 ©Paul Mountfort/Minecraft
Chapter 8:   Fig.5 ©Paul Mountfort

'FOR THE TIME WILL SOON COME WHEN HOBBITS WILL SHAPE THE FORTUNES OF ALL.'

GALADRIEL IN PETER JACKSON'S *THE FELLOWSHIP OF THE RING*